HOW TO PARTNER WITH GIRL SCOUT AMBASSADORS ON

YOUR VOICE YOUR WORLD

THE POWER OF ADVOCACY

IT'S YOUR WORLD—CHANGE IT! A LEADERSHIP JOURNEY

Girl Scouts of the USA

Grades 11-12

CHAIR,
NATIONAL BOARD
OF DIRECTORS

Patricia Diaz Dennis

CHIEF
EXECUTIVE
OFFICER

Kathy Cloninger

EXECUTIVE
VICE PRESIDENT,
MISSION TO MARKET

Norma I. Barquet

VICE PRESIDENT,
PROGRAM
DEVELOPMENT

Eileen Doyle

WRITERS: **Jennifer Goddard, Karen Unger, Monica Shah**

CONTRIBUTORS: **Laura Birnbaum, Kathleen Ferrier, Jan Herman,
Kate Gottlieb, Toi James, Maja Ninkovic**

ILLUSTRATED BY **Billie Jean**

DESIGNED BY **Parham Santana**

CONTENTS

"**What I like best is . . .** stepping back and watching the girls use the tools we have given them to find their own voice and lead."

—Shelly McIntosh, Girl Scout alumna and volunteer, Tempe, Arizona

A IS FOR *ADVOCACY,*
WHICH THIS JOURNEY IS ALL ABOUT.

You are about to guide the highest level of Girl Scouts to become advocates in their communities. Advocates get at the root of an issue. They zoom in on one critical angle of it and create a plan to address it. They then pitch that plan to those with the influence to make lasting change.

Advocacy is a public effort, but it has many personal components. Throughout this journey, the girls will have the opportunity to **develop valuable leadership skills**—problem-solving, research, networking, persuasive speaking, consensus-building. These are skills that will serve the Ambassadors throughout their lives—in their communities, their educational pursuits, their careers, and their families.

As they advocate for a cause they believe in, the Ambassadors will also **develop confidence**—confidence to shape policies and **become leaders who better the world.**

Advocacy: What It's All About

Webster's defines advocacy as "the action of pleading for or supporting." Whenever you try to persuade someone to do something or to see something your way, you are engaging in advocacy. Advocate comes from the Latin word for "voice." Being an advocate means to raise your voice to affect change.

When your group of Ambassadors goes out into the world as advocates, they will be joining a long line of women who have raised their voices for change throughout history. The girls' book features a time line of women advocates through the years. Encourage the Ambassadors to check it out, talk about it, be inspired by it, and perhaps even add to it. Who knows? Someday they may be part of it!

Advocacy in Girl Scouting

Since the founding of Girl Scouts in 1912 by Juliette Gordon Low, advocacy has been at the core of Girl Scouting. The organization's advocacy efforts range from influencing legislation to reaching out as a leading voice for girls at the federal, state, and local levels.

In recent years, the visibility of Girl Scouts as the preeminent advocacy organization for girls has increased around the nation, particularly on Capitol Hill. Successful advocacy efforts have included:

- Securing significant federal appropriations to reach underserved girls.

- Participating increasingly in policy dialogues as representatives of the interests of girls.

- Using the findings of the Girl Scout Research Institute to support the creation of public policies that benefit girls.

- Holding advocacy days in state capitals and the nation's capital, to inform and educate policymakers and community officials about issues that affect the Girl Scout organization or the rights of girls. In 2007, more than 700 Girl Scout members—girls and adults—met with legislators to advance the issue of healthy living among girls as part of GSUSA's Congressional Advocacy Day.

WORLDWIDE SISTERHOOD

GSUSA is a member of the World Association of Girl Guides and Girl Scouts (WAGGGS). This umbrella organization for our worldwide sisterhood, formed in 1928, advocates globally on issues of importance to girls and young women. For WAGGGS, advocacy means "speaking, doing, and educating." Learn more about WAGGGS at wagggs.org.

Advocacy may overlap with community service in many ways, but it is quite different from it. For a rundown on "Service, Action, and Advocacy," see page 29 in the girls' book.

Toward the Girl Scout Advocate Award

8 Steps to Advocacy

The road to advocacy can take many routes, but in this journey it follows eight sequential steps that the girls can easily fit into their busy lives—now and anytime they want to advocate. Each step builds on the one before, giving the girls new insights, stronger skills, and greater confidence.

The 8 Steps to Advocacy do not have to be accomplished in the exact order given in the Advocacy Central chart on pages 8–9, though that is likely the smoothest path to success. There are also no limits on the amount of time the girls can choose to spend on each step. They can take as much or as little time as needed. What's most important is for the Ambassadors to do what they find intriguing, exciting, and engaging.

First, though, they'll decide whether to journey forward on their own or as part of a team. If you're advising Ambassadors who are journeying solo, encourage them to collaborate as much as possible with friends, teachers, mentors, and other community members. Even those journeying with other Ambassadors may want to proceed with minimal adult guidance. Still, be ready to be needed. Even older teens can want, and flourish with, adult coaching and guidance.

No matter how Ambassadors travel through this journey, if they complete the 8 Steps to Advocacy, the prestigious Girl Scout Advocate Award is theirs.

The Girl Scout Advocate Award

AS YOU READ THROUGH THE 8 STEPS TO ADVOCACY, THINK ABOUT:

- Your own life experiences and what they've taught you about speaking up for what you believe in.

- People you know in the community and the connections they may have.

- Strengths, talents, and skills you possess that you can share with the girls.

Advocacy Central

The girls have an Advocacy Central section in their book, too, but instead of the Coaching Tips offered here, there's a column for all the details of their advocacy adventure—and separate charts to keep track of partners, VIPs, and tasks as their journey progresses. The girls' book also shows how one issue—getting more nutritious snacks into schools—could take shape through the 8 Steps to Advocacy." And don't worry. The sample sessions in this guide break down the advocacy steps even further, so you'll know exactly how to guide the girls all along the way.

	THE DETAILS	HOW TO ACHIEVE IT	COACHING TIPS
STEP 1: FIND YOUR CAUSE	Investigate issues you care about. Choose one that touches your heart and soul.	Stick to an issue you really care enough about to speak up for and act on—and to influence others to act on.	Encourage girls to consider a variety of issues before selecting their cause. By reading the news and networking with others, including Ambassadors, they'll get ideas about how to give voice to a problem and its solution. What issues are local officials tackling? Is there a cause many Ambassadors want to tackle together?
STEP 2: TUNE IN	Do some research. Zoom in on a specific angle and possible solutions.	Seek out the root causes. Where can you learn more? Consider as many sources of information as possible—the media, people in your community, the Internet. Are your sources trustworthy? Unbiased?	The girls need to choose one aspect of their cause and learn as much about it as possible. Guide them to be realistic about their available time. The more they can narrow their focus, the more successful they'll feel during the next steps. Researching the issue in the various ways listed in their book will let them zoom in on possible solutions. If working as a team, suggest that they divvy up the research and pool what they learn.
STEP 3: HARMONIZE	Form alliances with those who care about your issue and can assist you to give voice to solutions.	Find out who else is working on your issue. What advocacy efforts have been effective—or not so effective? Walk in the shoes of someone your issue impacts—or someone who can offer another perspective, perhaps even someone who has tried to address your cause without success. Gather with your partners and cooperate on the next steps.	As girls reach out to potential partners, remind them that this is a chance to practice networking skills. Partners might include organizations, local media, teachers, or college students already involved in the issue, even if just studying it. Even girls with limited time will benefit from a circle of partners—it's a chance to broaden their world. They might meet potential college and career contacts, so encourage the girls to keep a contacts list and to thank them all.
STEP 4: IDENTIFY THE BIG EARS AND SET UP A MEETING	Join with your partners to identify VIPs (very influential people) who will listen to you and have the influence to lift your cause.	Arrange to meet these VIPs. If possible, attend a public meeting (or two) where you can observe how your potential VIPs make decisions, handle issues, and promote their agenda. Is your issue on their radar? If not, find out how your VIPs take on "new business." Arrange a meeting. Get in touch via phone, e-mail, or a staff member.	The girls must decide who will listen to their analysis of the issue and influence change. As partners point out VIPs, coach girls to find the right VIPs. If they go to a local board only to find that their issue is a state one, they'll have spun their wheels. Asking questions along the chain of potential sources is critical. The more inquiries they make, the better. These critical thinking skills will benefit the girls all their lives. Step in to give background or get contacts rolling as needed, but keep the ball in the girls' court.

	THE DETAILS	HOW TO ACHIEVE IT	COACHING TIPS
STEP 5: **PREPARE YOUR PITCH**	Define your issue in a brief and compelling way, and propose a workable solution.	Say why your issue matters. Have a "hook." Propose a solution—make it reasonable, doable, and appealing to the VIPs. Clearly show the benefits—what's in it for you, me, and the community.	Girls want to be confident about speaking in public, so make time for the group to organize their presentation, and line up some practice audiences. Perhaps even identify a local expert (in PR or the media) who can provide tips.
STEP 6: **MAKE YOUR PITCH**	Make your pitch to the VIPs.	Use your confidence. This is it: Your Voice, Your World!	The girls will present their pitch to their VIP(s) and propose their solution. Cheer them on! Even if their pitch is not well received, remind the girls that they are still advocates, and that they are successfully moving through the steps to advocacy.
STEP 7: **CLOSE THE LOOP AND GIVE THANKS**	Now that you've done some great advocacy, acknowledge those you've met along the way and pass your efforts forward.	If VIPs jumped on board based on your pitch, use your thank-yous to detail your expectations of what they'll do next for your cause. If they're not on board, thank them for their time. Are you inspired to go further or have you done all you can? Either way, pass forward your good work—ideas, research, progress—to those who can move it forward even more (partners, school officials, other Girl Scouts, even your VIPs). Use what you've learned to educate and inspire others. How creative can you be in thanking those who supported your efforts?	Perhaps the girls are hooked and want to continue their efforts—by following up with their VIPs, identifying other VIPs, taking next steps suggested at their "pitch meeting," or devising a new approach. If they have the time, terrific! If not, they can "pass forward" any information, progress, or lessons learned to others who care about the issue, including partners and VIPs. All it may take is a note from the girls, reiterating possible solutions and next steps and saying thanks for their time. The important thing is to encourage the girls to be responsible and creative, so they truly "Close the Loop" and don't leave people or possibilities dangling.
STEP 8: **REFLECT, CELEBRATE**	Make sure you take time to reflect on your advocacy journey—all the bumps, valleys, high points, twists, and turns.	How did this effort make you wiser? How will you celebrate your new wisdom?	Plan some time for the girls to talk about what they have learned and how it applies not only to their journey experience, but to the rest of their lives. By sharing their insights, they'll gain new ideas for whatever lies ahead.

How Will Girls Choose an Advocacy Issue?

Some girls may care deeply about many issues: animal rights, global warming, child labor—any topic on people's minds or in the news. So they may need guidance on how to choose just one issue—and one angle of it. Other girls may not have given much thought to local and world issues. They may need their advocacy fire ignited. Community interviews, community mapping, and other research will let them uncover what they care about most.

Some girls may be uncomfortable contacting community officials or may not know how to start researching an issue. This book—and you—will guide them. Your goal is to advise girls on how to identify one aspect of an issue, and then offer any assistance and coaching they may need to network with potential partners and present their position to VIPs with the power to move a solution forward.

Don'ts (and Dos) to Keep in Mind

ELECTIONEERING: IT'S NOT ADVOCACY

Promoting candidates for elected office is not advocacy. In fact, laws governing non-profit organizations prohibit Girl Scouts from promoting candidates for office while acting as Girl Scouts. Learning when it is appropriate to express a personal point of view and when, as a representative of an organization, you may need to keep your opinions to yourself is a good life lesson for Ambassadors. It may be hard for a girl to understand why she can't campaign for a candidate who agrees with the issue she's advocating for. Make it clear that as an individual she can, but as a Girl Scout Ambassador she can't.

GIRL SCOUTS **MAY NOT:**		
Volunteer, perform ceremonies, or appear in uniform as a Girl Scout at any partisan event	Distribute fliers, posters, or other materials for a candidate	Raise money for any candidate or organization
Endorse candidates or speak publicly about candidates	Campaign against any candidate or political party	Make financial contributions from Girl Scouts to candidates or political parties

GIRL SCOUTS **MAY:**		
Take part in "get out the vote" activities (distributing registration forms, encouraging people to vote) as long as they're not favoring one candidate or cause	Assist voters in getting to polling places or provide activities for younger children at polling places	Organize mock elections at school
	Organize debates representing all sides	Create displays or other educational-awareness information about women in politics

Advocacy, Your Community, and You

On this journey, much depends on your community and how actively Ambassador-age teens are involved at its various levels of governance. If young people are not involved in the school board or local government at all, you might serve as an initial adult contact who explains the purpose of this Girl Scout program to the community's official bodies (those that might be involved in the girls' advocacy efforts). Once initial introductions are made, the girls can take over.

As the girls get their first taste of advocacy, they may become frustrated or demoralized if others disagree with them or if budgetary constraints or competing interests impede their progress—or if not many people care about their issue. Your life experience is critical here. The realization that even the smallest of gains can eventually foster much bigger changes may be hard for a teen to grasp. But, as an adult, you know that in real life the tortoise really often does win the race. Your steady assurance can keep the girls motivated.

Prep Work Counts

You may also find that girls are so excited by their chosen cause that they want to go straight to the top, bypassing the research, network-building, and other preparation needed before they pitch their ideas to VIPs. So encourage them to slow down. Let them know that slamming together a presentation likely won't do their cause justice.

FLEXIBILITY COUNTS

If the girls' efforts (calls, e-mails, letters, visits) are ignored, simply redirect the girls to new partners and VIPs, even if it means adjusting plans a bit and stretching out the advocacy time line.

CREATING A PERFECT PITCH INCLUDES YOU

The girls' book and this guide offer a wealth of information on how to create a polished pitch. Still, your life lessons and advice, and how you share them with the Ambassadors, can make a big difference between a winning pitch and a rejected one.

advocate

Scheduling the Journey

A is for assess. Take time to assess your viewpoint and your actions whenever you can. The Ambassadors will admire you for it. (That's another A!)

JUST HANGING OUT

There are no hard-and-fast rules about how much time Girl Scout Ambassadors spend exploring the topic of advocacy. Still, it's important to reserve some time for just hanging out. Emotional connections with other girls and a safe space to enjoy them are a key part of what makes Girl Scouting unique.

This guide outlines six sample sessions of approximately two hours each. Keep in mind that this is a journey packed with activities, information, and enriching experiences. As you create a schedule with your group of Ambassadors, you and the girls may want to stretch out the journey over a longer period of time than the sample sessions in this guide suggest. You may find you need more sessions—or shorter sessions or fewer sessions—that's for you and the girls to decide!

Encourage the girls to be creative about scheduling the journey. They might enjoy the intensity and bonding that could come from weekend retreats, regular after-school meetings, or intensive, summer-only sessions. Then again, meeting every two months for a full year may work best for some groups. Or the girls may want to explore some of the journey's suggested ideas and experiences on their own, gathering only periodically in person or online to discuss their thoughts.

Whatever the Pathway, the Award Is Within Reach

Even if girls are on a short pathway, they can still experience the steps of advocacy and earn an award as outlined in the sample sessions. Just be sure to coach the girls to focus on one angle of one issue, so they can create a realistic plan that engages them with at least one or two partners and VIPs.

FOLLOW A PRO

For a firsthand view of advocacy in action, encourage the girls to shadow an elected official or her staff member, or an advocate—anyone whose job involves advocacy (check out the career list on page 98 of the girls' book).

Roadside Attractions

As time allows, encourage the girls to "get off the highway" whenever possible to enjoy their own "roadside attractions." Stops can be "business" or "pleasure." Here are a few ideas (the girls' book and the Ambassadors themselves will have even more):

- Visit city hall, the seat of county government, or the state capitol to meet with elected officials and staff or to sit in on a meeting. While there, the girls can learn about the legislative process and how officials came to be in public office, what issues they work on, and how they practice leadership.

- Check out a local, state, or national advocacy effort such as Rock the Vote or Tree People.

- Find out if your Girl Scout council is engaged in advocacy efforts and how the girls might get involved.

- Discuss the pros and cons of a recent policy decision made at the local, state, or federal level. Maybe even conduct a debate. Why do the girls think the officials in charge decided as they did? What would the girls have done? Why?

- Visit places (such as a childhood home, sites of major speeches, or memorials) that honor an advocate the girls admire.

- Examine how stories about community issues are reported in the media, and analyze the various ways issues are portrayed.

- Visit colleges or universities in your region, where girls might sit in on classes related to their issues or see what students are advocating about.

- For guest speakers, invite a panel of experts, such as those advocating for the environment, health care, or other issues.

MAKE SOME STUFF

Girls who like to make things (crafts, recipes, do-it-yourself projects, inventions, crazy videos) will enjoy sharing their talents with the team. Encourage the girls to have fun as they share their favorite creative efforts. They can even exchange what they've made with each other. (Gifting ceremony, anyone?)

ENJOY THE OUTDOORS

Check out the camp properties offered by your Girl Scout council or local park facilities, and head out for some weekend retreats. Or go on a hike during which the girls share and debate solutions for their advocacy issue(s).

Sample Sessions at a Glance

SESSION 1

**Introduction,
Find Your Cause**

Girls learn about choices involved in the journey and begin to plan and schedule their journey and

- create a "girl-led" team agreement

- explore the meaning of advocacy and the steps involved, and the usefulness of advocacy in their lives

SESSION 2

**Community
Needs and
Personal Causes**

Girls identify their connections in their communities and

- use their ideas about community needs to explore possible areas for advocacy

- practice public speaking based on values of the Girl Scout Law

- consider trying on a "new mood" based on a personal outlook they want to practice

SESSION 3

**Tuning in
on an Issue**

Girls explore how their efforts could cause a "ripple effect" of action on their chosen issue and

- practice making realistic decisions based on their available time and, through research, break their issue down, "tuning in" to one specific angle of it

A is for adventure—the big one you are about to begin.

14

SESSION 4

**Building
a Network
of Partners**

Girls assess what they have learned about their issue and then create realistic solutions they will try to advocate toward and

- "harmonize" by identifying and beginning to reach out to partners who can strengthen their advocacy efforts

- develop team plans to "divvy up" next steps related to working with partners and identifying the "VIPs" who can act on their proposed solution

SESSION 5

**Reporting Back
on Partners and
Possible VIPs,
and Planning
the Perfect Pitch**

Girls assess and share progress mobilizing partners and identifying VIPs and

- explore the kinds of power and influence the VIPs they have identified could have on the issue/solution

- create and practice their presentation to VIPs

SESSION 6

**Closing
the Loop**

Girls assess the effectiveness of their pitch to VIPs and

- create plans for next steps or "closing the loop" so that their "butterfly effect" continues (whether or not they continue advocating)

- plan their own Opening Ceremony

SESSION 7

**Reflect, Reward,
Celebrate**

Girls reflect on what they have learned, felt and experienced on the journey and its impact on them and

- celebrate their experience based on their plans – perhaps even "passing it on" in some way to others

"**The rewards come as each girl accomplishes something she never thought she could.** The excitement in her conversation, the sparkle in her eyes—that is what makes being a Girl Scout volunteer worthwhile."

—Jane Pfaffenberger, Girl Scout volunteer and alumna, Avon, Indiana

YOU AND YOUR GROUP OF AMBASSADORS

Throughout this journey, you and the girls will gain deeper knowledge of one another and the rich traditions of Girl Scouting. So take some time to understand the likes and needs of Ambassador-age girls, and then dip into the traditions of Girl Scouts and the "what and how" of creating quality Girl Scout experiences.

As you read about the long-lasting leadership benefits of Girl Scouting, think about your own perspective on leadership. Your interest and enthusiasm are sure to be a driving force for the Ambassadors.

Understanding Ambassador-Age Girls

OPTIONS GALORE

For many girls in the final years of high school, every moment is crammed full—with preparing for tests, college, and careers, as well as socializing and just hanging with friends. Out of respect for this reality, this journey offers many options for how girls discover their voices, connect with others, and move forward to advocate for an issue of importance to them and the community at large.

SAMPLING "GIRL WORLD"

To get a read on issues important to 11th- and 12th-grade girls, spend some time in "girl world": Browse the magazine aisles of local stores to check out what's being read— good and not so good. Ask the girls for advice about surfing the Web and check out some of their favorite sites. Ask about movies, music, and TV shows, too, and then spend a little time watching and listening.

Teenage girls in the last two years of high school are almost young adults, and yet they're still girls. They love their growing independence, but they still need an adult to listen, give reassurance, and coach. They'll benefit from your experience and life skills. As you try to understand what may be going on in their hearts and heads, keep in mind that girls this age are:

Striving for a strong sense of self as they move out into the world, so don't let your own advocacy issues overshadow theirs. For example, suppose you've spent years working on cleaning up the river near your home or trying to curb wastewater. If one of the girls is focused on an environmental cause and wants to approach a government official who has not been open to your issues in the past, don't dissuade her—you never know, she may prove successful! Do advise her on others she can also approach, though, as she may need them.

Gaining independence and freedom, so they like to make their own decisions. That means they'll want activities and choices to be their own, even if it takes longer or may not be the path you would choose. For example, you may know that contacting a government official's office by phone is likely the best way to get an interview. But Ambassadors, who are probably IMing, text-messaging queens, may insist on sending an e-mail. Make suggestions, but then sit back and see what happens. If the interview comes through, fine. If not, a phone call can still be made, and the Ambassadors will have learned a lesson that will stick.

Craving friends to turn to and trust, and are eager to belong to trusted groups where they feel emotionally safe and connected. So emphasize how a major component of advocacy is reaching out and creating a network of alliances that will provide the safety net they need to further their causes. Plus, the "Take 5" activities in this journey are designed to give the girls breathers and time to hang out with friends.

Exploring risk-taking as a right of passage and managing the responsibilities of new privileges, such as driving. Let them know that advocacy involves risk-taking of the most positive kind—reaching out and taking responsibility for affecting change. This journey will let them express what they care about most deeply as they try to persuade those in positions of power to agree with them.

Juggling life decisions and pressures. Let them know that many skills they will practice as advocates are life skills that will serve them through college and their careers. Plus, advocacy builds self-confidence, which itself is the foundation for making smart decisions and withstanding peer pressure.

Communicating with Tech-Toting Ambassadors

You may be just as attached to cell phones and computers as the girls you're advising, but do you really know how important technology is to girls today? Consider these statistics:

- 93 percent of teens ages 12-17 use the Internet.[1]

- 51 percent of teens who use the Internet go online daily.[1]

- 55 percent of online teens have created online profiles (on sites such as MySpace or Facebook).[1]

- 60 percent of teens own two or three electronic gadgets.[1]

[1] Pew Internet and American Life Project 2007

GAUGING AMBASSADORS' NEEDS

As the Ambassadors explore advocacy, they'll be counting on you to be their biggest advocate. They'll want varying degrees of direction and advice. The girls may especially need your support and guidance to negotiate government meetings and other places they may not be familiar with. Advocacy expertise on your part isn't necessary. Just support them and cheer them on—and take pride as they mature into active, conscientious advocates.

FACE TIME COUNTS

As the girls seek out partners and then mobilize their network, they may reach for high-tech communications tools. Let them try it their way. But be ready to step in to gently encourage some good, old-fashioned communications methods, such as land-line telephones and face-to-face meetings.

What + How: Creating a Quality Experience

It's not just what girls do, but how you engage them that creates a high-quality experience. All Girl Scout activities are built on three processes that make Girl Scouting unique from school and other extracurricular activities. When used together, these processes—Girl Led, Cooperative Learning, and Learning by Doing (also known as Experiential Learning)—ensure the quality and promote the fun and friendship so integral to Girl Scouting. Take some time to understand these processes and how to use them with Girl Scout Ambassadors.

Girl Led

Being "girl led" is just what it sounds like: girls lead the planning and decision-making, especially at this highest level of Girl Scouting.

With Ambassadors, this means:

- **Girls will choose their issue.** If it's something large, such as global warming, guide them to consider how they can affect change locally by researching what is happening in their community that contributes to global warming.

- **Girls will research policy-making processes** in their community and beyond. Be prepared to offer guidance on how to identify resources that can help them. For example, you could assist them in locating local advocacy groups that are working for green solutions and give them tips on profiting from the contacts and information these groups already have.

- **Girls will decide how they want to schedule and conduct meetings**—whether monthly, weekly, or a more varied schedule, and whether in person, online, or by phone. Meetings can also vary in length depending upon the girls' time constraints. The substance of each meeting should also be girl led: Do they want sessions that are all business and some that are all fun, or do they want to mix it up? The girls can use the Ambassador meeting planner on pages 26–27 of their books to sketch out their meetings.

STEP BACK AND LET GO

As girls move through the steps to advocacy, consider "fading facilitation," a process in which your role decreases as the girls move deeper into their projects. The more they do, the more confident they become—and the less active you are. Your success is actually measured by how much you let go!

- **Girls will call, interview, and e-mail potential partners** to support their advocacy work—on their own. You can certainly offer suggestions (and maybe even nudge!), but let them make the contacts—unless they hit a roadblock and need you, as an adult, to make the inquiry.

- **Girls decide what "extras" to add** to their journey (field trips, retreats, outings, career explorations), even if it means just time to relax and recharge with sister Ambassadors. That is as valuable as the most educational road trip.

- **Girls decide whether and how they will partner** as a team. Some girls prefer to do their own thing; others work best in groups or with partners. They'll let you know which style they prefer.

Cooperative Learning

Through cooperative learning, girls work together toward shared goals in an atmosphere of respect and collaboration that encourages the sharing of skills, knowledge, and learning. Girls benefit from practicing teamwork, especially when they have different approaches to solutions. Working together in all-girl environments also encourages girls to feel powerful and emotionally and physically safe, and it allows them to experience a sense of belonging even in the most diverse groups.

Encourage the Ambassadors to engage in cooperative learning by:

- **Creating team goals** and working agreements. What do they want to do and by when? Who will do each part?

- **Negotiating a common ground** that includes everyone's ideas and goals. Reaching consensus on a joint project is an important life skill that they'll learn best on their own.

- **Working out conflicts** and seeking compromise. Conflicts are sure to crop up, and they'll learn conflict-resolution skills best by practicing them.

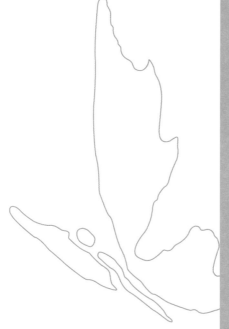

A is for aspirations, which this journey encourages.

- **Reaching out to the Girl Scout community** to team up with other Ambassadors in their region on the same issue or similar issues.

- **Identifying and connecting** with a network of partners who share their passion or have the ability to advance their message. A major part of this journey is the building of alliances and partnerships. Another is to unearth and then connect with VIPs. For these experiences, you are basically in the pit stop crew. So help change that flat tire quickly and get them back into the race.

- **Reflecting on their work** as a group and evaluating their progress—and then adapting plans as required. Teens may not always take the time needed to reflect on what they have accomplished or to assess what went well and what went wrong. Share your ability to evaluate your successes and failures, so the Ambassadors can gain these skills and see how and when to use them.

Learning by Doing

Girls gain fuller meaning from each experience when they take time to reflect on their actions. Although Ambassadors may feel they have so much to accomplish that they just want to "do," encourage them to stop and reflect, even when their efforts have a long time line. You might suggest that they:

- **Plan time at the end of each meeting to chat** about the activities they've just done. (You might prompt these discussions by asking something like: So why do you think we just did this?)

- **Chart their progress** and acknowledge and celebrate small milestones to keep them encouraged.

- **Celebrate big achievements**, too, and plan ceremonies for them.

Ceremonies and Traditions

Ceremonies are a great way to take time out of a busy day to share hopes, intentions, commitments, and feelings. Ceremonies mark a separation from whatever girls have just come from (school, work, dance class) and create the sense that what happens to them—together, as Girl Scout Ambassadors—is special and important.

Invite the girls to think about simple ways to mark their time together as special. One Girl Scout tradition that girls are never too old to enjoy is the friendship squeeze. It's often done as a closing ceremony at a meeting or at a campfire by first forming a Friendship Circle. Everyone gathers in a circle; each girl crosses her right arm over her left and holds hands with the people on either side. Once everyone is silent, the leader starts the friendship squeeze by squeezing the hand of the person to her left. One by one, each girl passes on the squeeze until it travels full circle. For a variation, invite girls to silently pass an affirmation or hope they have for each other as they pass the squeeze.

NOTHING FANCY NEEDED

Ceremonies can be as simple as forming a circle, lighting a candle, and sharing a hope, or reflecting together on one line of the Girl Scout Law. Girls might make their ceremonies more elaborate simply by reading poems, playing music, or singing songs.

Connecting with Family, Friends, and an Ever-Larger Circle

PLAN AHEAD

Thinking ahead to the journey's final session, check in early with the girls to see if they'd like to plan a celebratory event that lets their families and friends share their advocacy accomplishments.

Girl Scout Ambassadors will likely want to take trips and stay up late on retreats, and they may have a slew of fun ideas for the journey that they might like assistance with. Just remember, you don't have to be their only partner. Invite the girls' families and friends to get involved. Most important, encourage the girls themselves to think about who they can tap into. Mobilizing others, after all, is a key advocacy skill.

The girls might also expand their network by reaching across the region to other Girl Scout Ambassadors taking this advocacy journey. For example, girls from distinct areas—rural, suburban, and urban—might come together to share their advocacy efforts. They'll see how issues overlap or vary from one setting to another. And when teams of girls from various racial, ethnic, and socio-economic groups can share ideas, whether online or in life, they all stand to benefit. As advocates, they'll see how to think bigger about the collective power of their voices.

Expert Voices

Also think ahead with the girls about experts in the community who might add value to the journey, and plan ahead for visits with them. For example, a PR pro to help with "talking points" (a good prep step before the girls reach out to potential partners) is a good idea for Session 4 (see page 59), and various partners and VIPs could offer the girls perspectives on a range of careers, as suggested in Session 6 (page 77).

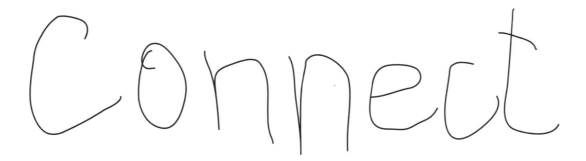

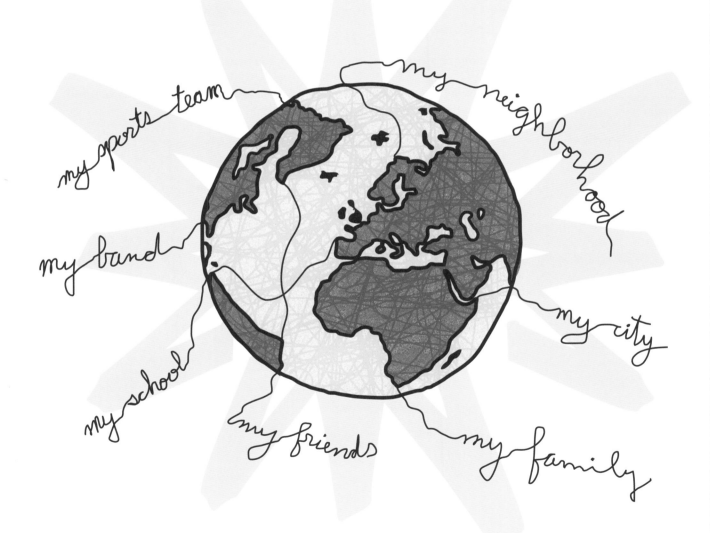

my sports team

my neighborhood

my band

my city

my school

my friends

my family

Safety and Well-Being

SAFETY-WISE

Keep this Girl Scout reference handy. It details the safety net provided for girls in Girl Scouting. Use it along with any additional information from your council to plan trips and outdoor activities, and to promote the well-being of the girls every time you get together.

CONTACT INFO FOR YOUR GIRL SCOUT COUNCIL

Name: _____
_____

Can help with:_____
_____
_____
_____

Phone: _____
E-mail: _____
_____

The emotional and physical safety and well-being of girls is of paramount importance in Girl Scouting. Look out for the safety of girls by following *Safety-Wise* when planning all gatherings and trips, and:

- following any guidelines your Girl Scout council might have, based on local issues.

- talking to girls and their families about special needs or concerns.

- creating an emotionally safe and trusting space for girls by partnering with them to make and stick to a team agreement.

- reminding girls not to disclose their names, addresses, or contact information when interacting online.

- calling on your Girl Scout council if you need additional expertise or referrals to community experts.

Welcoming Girls with Disabilities

Girl Scouting embraces girls with many different needs at all age levels, and is guided by a very specific and positive philosophy of inclusion that benefits all: Each girl is an equal and valued member of a group with typically developing peers.

As an adult volunteer, you have the chance to improve the way society views girls with disabilities. One way to start is with language. Your words have a huge impact on the process of inclusion. People-First Language puts the person before the disability.

SAY	INSTEAD OF
She has autism.	She's autistic.
She has an intellectual disability.	She's mentally retarded.
She has a learning disability.	The girl is learning-disabled.
She uses a wheelchair.	She is wheelchair-bound.
She has a disability.	She is handicapped.

Learn What a Girl Needs

Probably the most important thing you can do is to ask the individual girl or her parents or guardians what she needs to make her experience in Girl Scouts successful. If you are frank and accessible to the girl and her parents, it's likely they will respond in kind, creating a better experience for all.

It's important for all girls to be rewarded based on their best efforts—not completion of a task. Give any girl the opportunity to do her best and she will. Sometimes that means changing a few rules or approaching an activity in a more creative way. Here are a few examples:

• Invite a girl to perform an activity after observing others doing it first.

• Ask the girls come up with ideas on how to adapt an activity.

Often what counts most is staying flexible and varying your approach. For a list of online resources, visit www.girlscouts.org and search on "disability resources."

Understanding the Journey's Leadership Benefits

Though filled with fun and friendship, this Ambassador journey is designed to develop the skills and values girls need to be advocates in their own lives and in the world. "Girls advocate for themselves and others, locally and globally" is one of 15 national leadership outcomes, or benefits, of the Girl Scout Leadership Experience. Activities in this journey are designed to enable 10th- and 11th-grade girls to achieve seven of these outcomes, as detailed in the chart on the next page. You can notice the "signs" of these benefits throughout the journey.

Each girl is different, so don't expect them all to exhibit the same signs to indicate what they are learning along the journey. What matters is that the Ambassadors are developing leadership skills and qualities they can use right now—and throughout their lives.

For definitions of the outcomes and the signs that Girl Scout Ambassadors are achieving them, review the chart or see *Transforming Leadership: Focusing on Outcomes of the New Girl Scout Leadership Experience (GSUSA, 2008)*. Keep in mind that the intended benefits to girls are the cumulative result of traveling through an entire journey—and everything else girls experience in Girl Scouting.

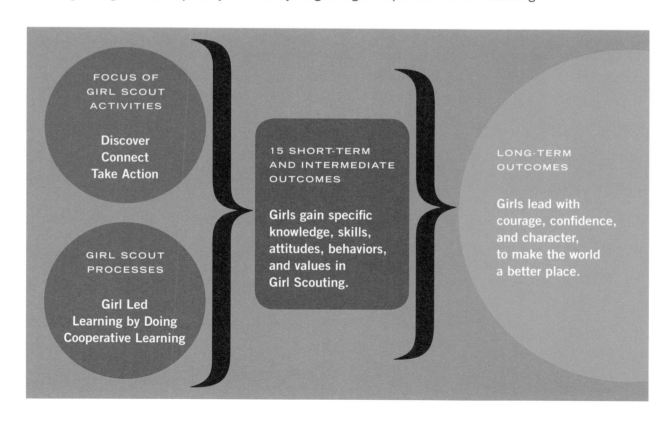

FOCUS OF GIRL SCOUT ACTIVITIES

Discover
Connect
Take Action

GIRL SCOUT PROCESSES

Girl Led
Learning by Doing
Cooperative Learning

15 SHORT-TERM AND INTERMEDIATE OUTCOMES

Girls gain specific knowledge, skills, attitudes, behaviors, and values in Girl Scouting.

LONG-TERM OUTCOMES

Girls lead with courage, confidence, and character, to make the world a better place.

NATIONAL LEADERSHIP OUTCOMES

		AT THE AMBASSADOR LEVEL, girls . . .	SAMPLE "SIGN" When the outcome is achieved, girls might . . .	EXAMPLES of how the outcome plays out in this journey
DISCOVER	**Girls develop positive values.**	act consistently with a considered and self-determined set of values.	choose educational and career goals in line with the values they consider important.	Girls' advocacy issues reflect their values and allow them to "live" their values.
DISCOVER	**Girls seek challenges in the world.**	have increased confidence to discuss and address challenging issues and contradictions in their lives and in their local and global communities.	look for ways personal habits conflict with achieving goals that are important to them (e.g., fighting global warming).	The journey offers many challenges—reaching out to new people, speaking up, being assertive.
CONNECT	**Girls promote cooperation and team-building.**	are able to promote cooperation and effective team-building in their communities.	describe how their advocacy efforts encouraged sustained cooperation among various people and/or organizations in their communities.	Girls organize partners—in team-building that may go far beyond girl-to-girl or peer teamwork.
CONNECT	**Girls feel connected to their communities locally and globally.**	have extensive feelings of connection with their local and global communities.	place high value on providing support for diverse members of their communities.	Girls take on issues and meet others in the community in the process.
TAKE ACTION	**Girls can identify community needs.**	are more skilled in identifying issues that balance feasibility with achieving long-term changes in their local or global communities.	identify community partners that can continue their project goals into the future.	The first two steps to advocacy compel girls to think of root causes of a community issue. Selecting VIPs makes them consider who owns the issue and who can influence change.
TAKE ACTION	**Girls advocate for themselves and others.**	actively seek partnerships with other organizations that provide support and resources for their advocacy efforts.	report working with organizations that share their advocacy goals.	The whole advocacy process.
TAKE ACTION	**Girls feel empowered to make a difference.**	feel their projects and ideas are valued/respected by stakeholders in their local and/or global communities.	give examples of positive reports about their advocacy efforts.	The "8 Steps to Advocacy" allow girls to break down the advocacy process and feel confident at each step along the way.

Your Perspective on Leadership

The Girl Scout Leadership philosophy—Discover + Connect + Take Action—implies that leadership happens from the inside out. Girls discover their skills and values as leaders, and then connect with others to take action to better the world. This philosophy stresses the importance of working collaboratively with others to make things better for everyone. In Girl Scouts, a leader is not simply someone in a position of authority or someone who likes to be "in charge."

Before starting on this leadership journey, take some time to think about your own view of leadership. Your beliefs and values, and your attitude—about leadership and the advocacy efforts encouraged by this journey—will have an impact on the girls. Try the following reflection exercise and revisit it throughout the journey. You may even find it useful to network with fellow volunteers and share ideas about your progress guiding girls through this advocacy journey.

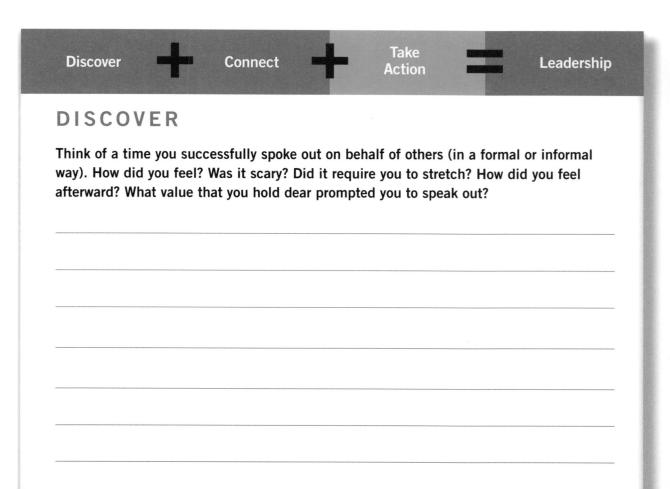

Discover **+** Connect **+** Take Action **=** Leadership

DISCOVER

Think of a time you successfully spoke out on behalf of others (in a formal or informal way). How did you feel? Was it scary? Did it require you to stretch? How did you feel afterward? What value that you hold dear prompted you to speak out?

How can you use your insights to coach girls to find where their values might intersect with a cause they can speak up for?

_____

_____

_____

_____

CONNECT

How has your network of connections helped you in life? Think of a time when you reached out and made some new connections. Was it difficult? Scary? Was it worth it?

_____

_____

_____

How can you guide girls to expand their networks as they venture through this journey?

_____

_____

_____

TAKE ACTION

Let your imagination run wild: Suppose this generation of young women were to put its advocacy skills to work in every aspect of their lives—how might the world be better? How can you convey your hopes to the girls?

_____

_____

_____

"What I like best about guiding is taking a young lady from a baby through to adulthood. I like to think of them as 'diamonds' in the rough."

—Debbie Esposito, Girl Scout volunteer and alumna, Roselle, New Jersey

THE JOURNEY'S 7 SAMPLE SESSIONS

For the seven sample sessions in this guide, sample is truly the key word. They are suggestions only. The sample sessions draw on the information in the girls' book to engage the Ambassadors in team discussions, experiences, and reflections. Each session consists of activities that lead to or satisfy the various steps the girls need to complete to earn the Advocate Award. Sessions also include optional activities that offer fun team-building exercises or meeting energizers that tie to advocacy. The sample sessions show how you and the girls can link experiences together, creating the feeling of being on a journey that is bigger and more important than any one activity on its own.

Looking Ahead

Before each meeting, read the appropriate section of the girls' book and make sure you have the **supplies you need**. Jot down (perhaps on newsprint or index cards) **notes and questions to ask** the girls to assist them in reaching their goals. Take a moment after each session to **think about next steps**, and **write down any "to-dos"** that come to mind. **Check in with the girls about any ideas they might have.**

Before you can score,
you must first have a goal.

—Greek proverb

SAMPLE SESSION 1
Introduction, Find Your Cause

AT A GLANCE

Goal: Girls begin creating and leading their own advocacy experience as a team.

(Experiences and discussions related to the introductory section and Step 1 in the girls' book)

- Welcome and Introductions
- Ceremony
- Overview of the Journey
- Make It Yours

- Girl-Led Guidelines
- Looking Ahead to Session 2: Toward Choosing a Cause
- Closing Ceremony (optional)

ADVOCATES IN POP CULTURE

To add some cultural flair to the advocates the girls have in their book, dip into popular culture from time to time. The arts, for example, are filled with inspiring women, real and fictional. Here are a few you may remember. Talk about them—and any others you can think of—with the Ambassadors throughout the journey. Encourage the girls to seek out current cultural figures. Perhaps they'll want to create their own pop culture time line of women advocates.

1970 MARY TYLER MOORE is single, 30, and just getting over her ex-boyfriend. Sorry, make that Mary Richards, the independent career woman Moore plays in "The Mary Tyler Moore Show." When Mary tosses her hat in the air—the classic opening for the credits—she's tossing a lot more than her hat, namely all the conventional expectations that women, single women especially, have lived by. The show is so popular and the character so beloved that Mary may have done more for women's liberation than all the decade's radical feminists combined.

1972 HELEN REDDY records the song "I Am Woman," which sells more than a million copies and reaches No. 1 on the Billboard charts. The song not only wins a Grammy Award, propelling Reddy to stardom, it strikes a chord with feminists of the '70s. Lyrics like "I am woman, hear me roar / In numbers too big to ignore" and "I am strong / I am invincible / I am woman" reflects a new mood of confident women.

1988 MURPHY BROWN arrives on the tube in the sitcom "Murphy Brown." An update of Mary Richards, who worked in a newsroom, Murphy is the star reporter for a TV newsmagazine and a recovering alcoholic who faces more challenges in her personal life than Mary ever dreamed of. Played for 10 years by Candace Bergen, she takes on everything from divorce to breast cancer. When Murphy undergoes chemotherapy, there's a reported 30 percent increase in mammogram testing. Talk about making a difference . . .

1988 ROSEANNE BARR stars as an overweight mom who "wears the pants" in the family on the hit TV sitcom "Roseanne." She puts such a funny spin on the life of her working-class family that the show manages to address serious topics with ground-breaking candor but without offending its prime-time audience. Roseanne and her Midwestern brood keep viewers glued to their TVs for nine years.

Welcome and Introductions

Congratulate the girls on being Girl Scout Ambassadors who are ready to explore the world of advocacy. Then briefly introduce yourself (30 seconds or less!), and add one interesting personal tidbit ("My favorite show is . . . "). Next, ask the girls to go around the group and do the same. If the girls already know each other well, simply "up" the introductions a notch: Suggest that each girl ask one other girl a question—a positive one!—so the entire group will learn something new and interesting about each girl.

Ceremony

Invite the girls to consider the importance of ceremony in their lives—hugs when they see friends or family, school dances, high-fives, graduations, and the like. Girl Scouting has a long history of ceremonies: reciting the Girl Scout Promise, telling stories around a campfire, making S'mores, trading SWAPS.

Ask the girls if they would like to take five minutes right now to come up with an opening (or closing) ceremony to mark the day's session or a future session. If the girls' opinions are mixed, ask how they might reach a group decision. For the ceremony, you might offer a few suggestions:

Share a wish for the world, or this journey. The opening ceremony could be a fun way for the girls to play up the significance of the butterfly, the powerful symbol of transformation mentioned in this journey. Share with them how the butterfly is a key element in Native American legends, which say that if you have a secret wish, you should capture a butterfly and whisper your wish to it. Butterflies don't speak, so your secret is ever safe in its keeping. When you release the butterfly, giving it back its freedom, your wish will be granted.

Ask the girls if they want to begin each meeting by writing a wish, either on a butterfly shape cut from paper that they place between the pages of their journey books as keepsakes, or on dried leaves that they "release" into the wind so their messages are carried into the world.

SWAPS

Trading SWAPS (Special Whatchamacallits Affectionately Pinned Somewhere) is a beloved Girl Scout tradition of exchanging small keepsakes. It started long ago when Girl Scouts and Girl Guides from England first gathered for fun, song, and making new friends. Swaps are still a fun way for Girl Scouts to meet and promote friendship. Each swap offers a memory of a special event or a particular girl. A swap usually says something about a Girl Scout's group or highlights something special about where she lives. And it's simple—it could be made from donated or recycled goods.

Choose a woman who inspires. The girls might want to start meetings by sharing with the group their thoughts about one of the women advocates featured in the time line in their books and saying why she is inspiring. The girls can even kick this idea up a notch by thinking about a future time line. Suggest that they imagine that the year is 2038. What does each girl think the advocacy time line will say about her then?

Sing a song, recite a poem. The girls might want to open their meeting with a song or a poem. For example, they might want to sing an empowering or inspiring song (Alicia Keys's "No One," Lee Ann Womack's "I Hope You Dance," or John Lennon's "Imagine") or one that features butterflies (see sample lyrics below). The girls are sure to have plenty of ideas of their own from the music they listen to.

Best,
You've got to be the best
You've got to change the world
And you use this chance to be heard
Your time is now

—from "Butterflies and Hurricanes," by Muse

A is for affirm—affirm the progress the Ambassadors make as they strive to create positive change in their world.

Overview of the Journey

Advocacy vs. Service: Advocacy is this journey's theme, and it's important for the Ambassadors to understand the full force of advocacy and how it differs from community service, which they may have experience with. Check out the "Service, Action, and Advocacy" section that begins on page 27 of the girls' book.

- Ask: *In what ways have you served the community?* If the girls need a jump-start, offer some examples of formal community service (volunteering at a local hospital or animal shelter) and informal service (raking leaves for an elderly neighbor, volunteering at church).

- Then ask the girls to define advocacy. If needed, offer a definition: *Advocacy is when you get to the root of important issues and propose solutions for positive, long-lasting change in the community and beyond.*

- Engage the girls in the reflection on page 30 of their books: *Think of a time you provided service. How could you have lifted that service to advocacy?* Ask the girls to share their answers.

- If there's time, try the reflection on page 32 of the girls' book, "How Influential Are You?" Ask the girls how they scored, and perhaps have them share how many items they checked. Is there one item all are involved in? Any item none are involved in?

8 Steps to Advocacy: Next, invite the girls to discuss the "8 Steps to Advocacy" chart in Advocacy Central (pages 8–9 in this guide and 10–11 in the girls' book), making it clear that this is the heart of the journey—it lays out the steps to advocacy and is the Ambassadors' ticket to a prestigious Girl Scout award.

Ask the girls some questions, such as:

- Which steps seem the most interesting to you? Which step do you most look forward to?

- Which steps might seem a little hard?

- Do you have any concerns about any of the steps? If so, how might you overcome them?

- Be sure to emphasize how useful the steps can be in all areas of life. Ask the girls to think about instances in which they might be useful even if they are not advocating for an issue.

- Ask: *How will doing the steps help you stretch and grow—not just as an advocate but in all walks of life?*

Make It Yours

Now is a good time for the girls to consider the "Make It Yours" reflection on page 22 of their book (and reprinted below), which asks them to think of any personal goals they might accomplish on this journey.

- Ask them to share any personal hopes and goals they may already have in mind for this journey, and encourage them to think more deeply about possible goals before they write them in their books.

- Sharing their goals and where they are in achieving them can possibly be a meaningful component of any future opening or closing ceremonies they create.

IF YOUR GROUP IS LARGE

The girls could pair up or create small teams to share their goals—it's another way for them to get to know one another better.

Make it yours.

Any personal goals waiting on your plate? Things to help jump-start the rest of your life—school projects or college interviews and applications? Can you accomplish any of them on this advocacy adventure? How about improving your community *and* becoming a better public speaker? Or sharpening your persuasive writing skills? Hit the gym more often? Stop procrastinating?

Chat about possible goals with your friends. Get their advice.

Use the space below to jot down anything you want to accomplish on this journey. Visit this page every so often to add in or check off!

I want to _____

_____

_____ says to try _____
(friend's name)

_____

AIM FOR VARIETY

Although some Ambassadors may be determined to race toward an award, encourage the group to plan sessions that are flexible and varied—with some time devoted to the "heavy lifting" of advocacy and some to their chosen "roadside attractions" and team-building exercises. And don't forget all the extra fun factors, including breaks for energizing snacks or just to hang out.

A is for adapt. Everything may not go as planned, so keep this in mind: flexibility is an admirable quality for Ambassadors and advisers.

Girl-Led Guidelines

Suggest that the Ambassadors start to think about some journey guidelines and perhaps even a team agreement. You might say something like, *Let's set up some guidelines for how we'll work together to build on our commonalities and strengths and maximize our efforts as a team of advocates.*

• Ask the girls to focus on basic guidelines for how they'll work together on the journey, such as, "Don't interrupt," "Respect others' opinions," "Ask to hear opinions from all girls," and the like. Encourage the girls to consider all ideas before rejecting any.

• Ask for a volunteer to chart the group's ideas. This will encourage the girls' ownership of the guidelines. You can then post the chart at each meeting and refer to it as necessary—for example, during debates or disagreements.

Once their guidelines are written, invite the girls to begin to shape plans for the journey. Talk about meeting times, taking notes, doing activities outside of sessions, planning trips, and their level of interest in earning the Advocate Award. Now might be a good time for the girls to start using the Your Voice, Your World planner on pages 26–27 of their book.

shout it out for advocacy

Looking Ahead to Session 2:
Toward Choosing a Cause

Before the girls choose their cause, it will be helpful for them to decide if they want to work as one or two large groups on one issue or divide into smaller teams so they can advocate on a few issues. This is a good chance for them to reach out into the Girl Scout community and network with other Ambassadors who are advocating on issues in the region. Encourage girls to discuss both the pros (the power of team work, especially for maximizing their time and effort) and possible cons (they may have to compromise on their cause) of advocating as a group.

Suggest that the girls communicate with each other outside the session as they gather information about various issues. They can do some trend-spotting by talking to family, neighbors, friends, school administrators, and teachers and by keeping up with daily news of their community and the world, whether through papers, online sites, or TV. What issue can they focus on that fits into the rest of their lives?

Once the girls have done some community research, they can fill out the "What Pulls Your Heartstrings?" chart on page 42 of their book and then try the Reflection and Passion-Meter exercises that follow. These are great starting points for the group discussions of communities and community issues in Session 2.

Closing Ceremony:
A is for Advocates (optional)

Offer the final few minutes of the session for the girls to hold their first closing ceremony. If they don't have anything planned, ask them if they've noticed all the fun "A is for . . ." and "B is for . . ." lines in their book. Suggest that they choose their own letter of the alphabet and come up with their own list of "is fors" to express their hopes for this journey. They can do it as a group, with each girl writing one line, or as individuals, with each girl writing a set of lines. Either way, encourage the Ambassadors to have fun and share their "is fors" with each other—either at the next session or right now and as an impromptu closing that can be continued at future sessions, adding a few lines at each step along the journey so that by its end, the Ambassadors have a complete group poem.

MAPPING FOR A CAUSE

The next chapter of the girls' book, "Step 1: Find Your Cause" (page 36), offers a key way for the girls to focus in on an issue worth advocating for—community mapping. The girls may wish to start a discussion of the communities they belong to now, and then think about them further, wrapping up their discussion at the next meeting.

GO MOBILE WITH RESEARCH

If the Ambassadors live in a village, town, or city, you may be able to do some "walk-around" community research as a group during the session. You could even go to a mall to observe and interview people. Or members of the community could be invited to the next meeting to offer their views on critical issues. It's up to your group of Ambassadors!

"If you don't like the way
the world is, you change it.
You have an obligation to change it.
You just do it one step at a time."

—Marian Wright Edelman

SAMPLE SESSION 2
Community Needs and Personal Causes

AT A GLANCE

Goal: Girls use their values and community connections to choose an advocacy issue for their journey.

(Continues the experiences and discussions in Step 1 of the girls' book and moves into Step 2)

- Opening Ceremony (optional)
- Community Connections and the Community Pretzel
- Reflection and Decision
- Advoca-Ts

- Public Speaking and the Girl Scout Law
- Take 5: The Many Moods of You
- Looking Ahead to Session 3
- Closing Ceremony (optional)

MATERIALS

- List of communities the girls in your group will relate to, such as sports, school, Girl Scouts, etc.
- Newsprint
- Colored markers

Opening Ceremony (optional)

If the girls took to having opening ceremonies, invite them to open their gathering. If nothing formal was planned, invite them to go around and say what mood they bring to today's gathering. Or they might share the best or worst part of their day so far, or some other little way of connecting.

Community Connections and the Community Pretzel

Next, suggest that the girls play Community Pretzel, a fun, physical game sort of like Twister that will get them talking once again about the community connections they started exploring in the first session. The girls may even want to lead this game themselves, or they may suggest substituting another activity that gets them thinking about their connections. Here's the basic concept for Community Pretzel:

- The girls stand in a circle within arm's reach of one another.

- The "caller" (either you or a girl) says a type of community (for example, 11th grade or the basketball team or the French Club) and asks the girls to connect one part of their clothing or their body with the same part of another member of that community. For example, If you are a member of the sports-playing community, place the sides of your shoes together. Or, if you are a member of a religious community, touch one of your knees with a knee of another member of that community. Girls are to remain connected throughout the game.

- Start by having the girls connect in small ways—pinkies, shirtsleeves, wrists, ankles—so you have plenty of options to work through before you run out of the basics like hands, feet, knees, elbows, ears, shoulders, and backs.

- By the time you get halfway down the list, you may have a giant pretzel of giggling girls standing before you. Ask if they want you to keep going. Their level of comfort with physical proximity and contact may be reaching its limit!

SILLINESS: NOT EVERYONE'S S'MORE

Even though Ambassadors are young women, they may enjoy opportunities to be a little silly. But if that's not the mood of the group, feel free to adjust your activities. For example, the girls might find another way to creatively map their community connections, like making a crazy-quilt map on paper of all the ways their communities intersect.

While girls are still in the Community Pretzel formation, ask, *What does this tell you about communities?* (Possible answers: *We're all part of them, We're all interconnected,* or *We can belong to the same community as someone we didn't think we had a lot in common with*).

After the Ambassadors untangle themselves, invite them to discuss how the Community Pretzel can be viewed as a physical representation of the group's shared communities. Did they notice how their various communities varied in size? Were they surprised by the size of any of the communities or by the members of those communities? Were there any communities they don't belong to but wish they did?

Next, steer the discussion toward advocacy:

• Ask: **What does the idea of community connectedness have to do with advocacy?** (Possible answers might include: *We can tap into a lot of different communities when we act as advocates. We can connect with other advocates in our communities. Our advocacy causes might stem from what matters in our communities.*)

• Next, give each girl a colored marker, and ask all the girls to take a turn writing what communities they are members of on a large piece of newsprint. If more than one girl writes the same community (such as Ambassadors, their grade in school, etc.), have them use arrows or bubbles to connect them.

• Then ask the girls to use a different colored marker to write the issues they have heard expressed in each community they have just noted. (Remember, they were going to do some community research ahead of this session.) The resulting "community map," which will reveal what's happening in their various communities, will aid them as they focus their advocacy efforts.

The "What Pulls Your Heartstrings?" chart on page 42 of the girls' book is now essential for the girls to complete so they can close in on their advocacy issue for the journey. The girls may want to divide into pairs or smaller groups or spend some time individually filling out their charts. Just ask them how they might be most comfortable and productive. Then, as a group, they might follow up with the Reflection and Passion-Meter activities—unless they had time to enjoy those activities together in Session 1.

A is for add them up—all the benefits this journey offers girls!

Reflection and Decision

Engage the girls in a discussion of the reflection questions on page 47 of their book. And perhaps add a few more to get them going:

• Which idea do you like most?

• Which idea might be the most possible to do?

• Which idea might help you learn the most?

• Which idea affects you personally?

• Which idea is most critical to your community?

Guide the discussion so that girls narrow their ideas to the one issue (or a few issues, if the group has split into small teams) they will advocate for during the rest of the journey. As the team comes to a decision, encourage the girls to check in on their team agreement (from Session 1). How are they doing? Is it hard or easy to make a team decision? Why?

Public Speaking and the Girl Scout Law

Ask each girl to decide which line of the Girl Scout Law not only most resonates with her but also best represents advocacy. After 10 minutes of prep time, each girl (or the Ambassadors can do this in pairs, if they like) has one minute to speak to the group and present her case in a persuasive and professional manner. Encourage the girls to get creative with visuals, statistics, or anything else they choose. The fun factor of this can be upped a few notches by writing the lines of the Girl Scout Law on slips of paper, placing them in a bag or bowl, and letting each girl (or pair of girls) pick one. After a little preparation, each girl or pair delivers a pitch.

Take 5: The Many Moods of You

Use the "Discover the Many Moods of You" Take 5 break, on page 41 of the girls' book, as a fun way to wind down and close out the session. Talk about the activity, then have each girl pick the mood she plans to feature on her ring, key chain, bookmark, or other item. Or maybe the girls want to think up their own twist on the activity and make a mood item on their own with friends, as suggested. But if they're itching to make it in this session, and you have the time, chime in and let the girls know what mood you are going to try out!

ELIMINATING SPEAKER'S JITTERS

Practicing persuasive public speaking is important for the Ambassadors because girls their age frequently say that public speaking is scary. Incorporating short and simple ways for them to practice speaking in front of others can help get them over any initial jitters. Close out the pitching with a discussion to wrap up how the advocacy effort of this journey is connected to the Girl Scout Law.

A IS FOR ACTING, AS IN IMPROV

Up the fun factor of the persuasive speaking by asking the girls to take turns being the "expert" on some made-up topics. Each girl has exactly one minute to speak off-the-cuff about her topic, which she pulls from a bag (or box or hat). Sample topics might be:

• The Origin of the Banana Split

• Why Unicorns Make Great Pets

• How to Build an Internal Combustion Engine from Garbage

• Our Hometown Is the New Fashion Capital of the World!

Looking Ahead to Session 3

If possible, make plans to hold Session 3 at a location where the girls will have access to research resources, such as a school computer room or library, the local public library, or a place with Internet and phone access. Ask the girls to suggest the meeting place that would best satisfy their research needs. A government office building with archives or a college library may be even more interesting. A well-resourced location will allow the girls to begin their research—and it will be more fun if they can do it together.

Closing Ceremony (optional)

Allow time for the girls to perform a closing ceremony—if they had one planned or if they want to create an impromptu one.

ADVOCA-TS

Now that the girls have their cause selected, they might want to brainstorm some catchy slogans for it. Up the fun factor of slogan writing with Advoca-Ts, the T-shirt-making project suggested on page 84 of the girls' book. The girls might enjoy wearing the shirts as they research their cause in Session 3.

SAMPLE SESSION 3
Tuning in on an Issue

AT A GLANCE

Goal: Girls make a team decision and focus in on one realistic angle of their advocacy issue.

(Experiences and discussions from Step 2 of the girls' book)

- Opening Ceremony (optional)
- The Butterfly Effect
- Time Crunch
- Researching the Issue
- Take an Assessment Break
- Discover Your Inner Child
- Closing Ceremony (optional)

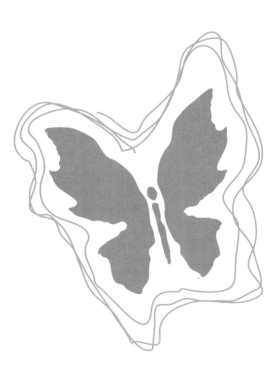

Opening Ceremony (optional)

Give the girls time to conduct their opening ceremony. If none was planned, ask for volunteers to lead an impromptu ceremony to mark this time together as special.

The Butterfly Effect

Have the girls refer to page 6 of their book and read the quote from Kofi Annan that introduces the "Butterfly Effect," the theory that an action as small and seemingly inconsequential as the fluttering of a gossamer butterfly wing can eventually lead to large-scale weather phenomena elsewhere on the planet.

According to this theory, small, positive changes, such as local advocacy efforts, can lead to history-altering change in the world at large. A good example is the effect Rosa Parks, a seamstress in Montgomery, Alabama, had in December 1955, when she refused to give up her seat on a city bus to a white passenger. Parks was certainly aware of the immediate consequences of her actions—arrest and a fine for violating a city ordinance. But she couldn't have known that her small act would lead to a chain of increasingly larger reactions and actions that affected the entire struggle for civil rights and led to her being called "the mother of the civil rights movement."

Ask the girls to imagine the impact of thousands of Girl Scout Ambassadors around the world, each making one small change. Can they think of an example of the Butterfly Effect in their own lives, or in their communities? Then, to emphasize how small acts can have a great impact, gather the group together for the following game, which can be played indoors or out:

Butterfly Chain-Tag

This activity is designed to get the Ambassadors thinking about the Butterfly Effect on a local scale, and possibly in a more personal way. If the girls are feeling more low key, they can choose to skip the game's physical aspect (linking arms) in favor of creating a group story or poem that they write on newsprint or a chalkboard. Read the scenarios given on the next page for ways the game can unfold, and then walk the girls through these steps:

- Ask a girl to volunteer to be "it." She will then mention a small (positive, negative, or neutral) action she performed that day (put on strawberry lip gloss, ate a burger at a fast-food joint, talked for an hour on her cell phone) and then "tag" another girl.

- She and the tagged girl link arms. The tagged girl must now come up with an effect that could result from the first girl's action.

- The second girl then tags a third girl, who must come up with an effect of what the second girl said.

- And so on through the entire group until all the girls are linked.

THE THEORY AND ITS ORIGIN

The Butterfly Effect was named by meteorologist Edward Lorenz, who spoke about it first in 1963 at the New York Academy of Sciences, using the example of the flap of a seagull's wing ("If the theory were correct, one flap of a seagull's wings would be enough to alter the course of the weather forever"). He spoke about it again in 1972 at a meeting of the American Association for the Advancement of Science in Washington (by then, a butterfly had replaced the seagull).

Encourage the girls to play a second (or even a third) round so that another girl can start off the game with a new action.

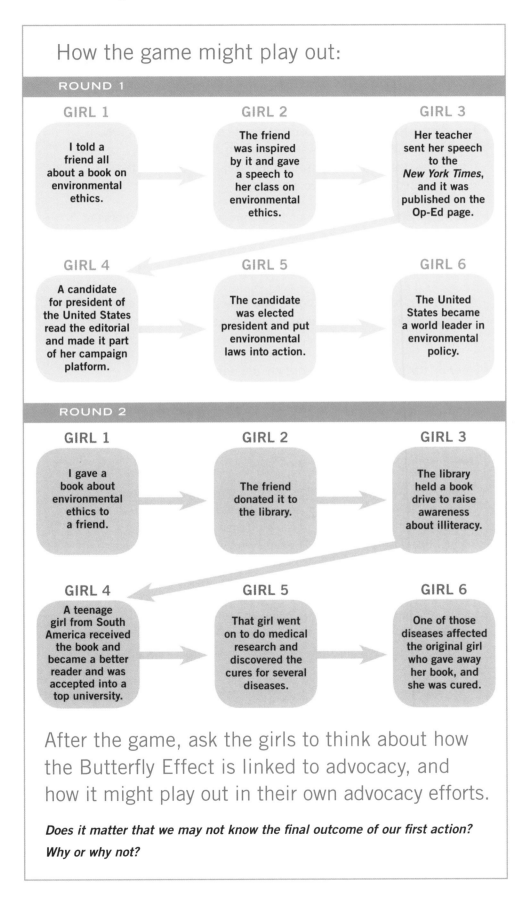

How the game might play out:

ROUND 1

GIRL 1
I told a friend all about a book on environmental ethics.

GIRL 2
The friend was inspired by it and gave a speech to her class on environmental ethics.

GIRL 3
Her teacher sent her speech to the *New York Times*, and it was published on the Op-Ed page.

GIRL 4
A candidate for president of the United States read the editorial and made it part of her campaign platform.

GIRL 5
The candidate was elected president and put environmental laws into action.

GIRL 6
The United States became a world leader in environmental policy.

ROUND 2

GIRL 1
I gave a book about environmental ethics to a friend.

GIRL 2
The friend donated it to the library.

GIRL 3
The library held a book drive to raise awareness about illiteracy.

GIRL 4
A teenage girl from South America received the book and became a better reader and was accepted into a top university.

GIRL 5
That girl went on to do medical research and discovered the cures for several diseases.

GIRL 6
One of those diseases affected the original girl who gave away her book, and she was cured.

After the game, ask the girls to think about how the Butterfly Effect is linked to advocacy, and how it might play out in their own advocacy efforts.

Does it matter that we may not know the final outcome of our first action? Why or why not?

GAME OPTIONS

The game can also be played with more serious actions, such as "There's an oil spill off the coast of California" or "A child gets bullied and beaten up by a 10th-grader." Let the girls decide if they want to go for fun/silly or significant/serious—or mix it up and do rounds of each.

Time Crunch

Invite the girls to check out the "Make It Yours" time-crunch activity on page 53 of their books. The idea is to create a visual representation of the group's time commitments so they can see how precious their time is on the advocacy journey and how important it is to "work smart." The chart the girls create together can serve as a "reality check" in setting realistic goals.

- Use chart paper (or a chalkboard) to create a larger version of the chart below. There are 480 waking hours in a month—720 total hours, less the 240 girls need for sleeping if they get the recommended 8 hours of zzzs every night.

- Ask the girls to say the activities they do regularly over the course of a "normal" month (such as homework and studying, playing sports, after-school club meetings, hanging out with friends, doing chores, going to work, spending time with family).

- Ask the girls to guesstimate how much time they spend on each activity (multiply this number as needed to get the total amount for the month).

- After all the girls have reported, total the number of hours committed, and then subtract that number from 480. Remember, this is a representation of the group's availability, not the availability of individual girls. If girls have elected to work independently on the advocacy journey, doing this activity is still helpful and recommended.

- Don't be surprised if the number is negative—it's a valuable wake-up call to acknowledge that girls this age are often stretched to the limit time-wise. Ask: *Where do you get those extra hours to accomplish all these things?* Their answers will most likely cause them to admit that they skip on sleep or relaxation time.

- Ask girls to reflect on what this means for them as a group (with regard to teamwork, delegating tasks, and time management). How much time can they realistically commit to seeing through the project? Are any adjustments necessary?

ACTIVITY:	AMOUNT OF TIME:
Sleep	240 hours
School (8 hours per day, 5 days per week)	160 hours
TOTAL HOURS: _____	
TIME REMAINING: _____ (subtract total from 480)	

A is for ask—ask the Ambassadors questions whenever you can.

Researching the Issue

Ask the girls to think about their chosen advocacy issue by considering the following questions:

- *How much do I know about the issue? Do I know its history?* (What has already been done? Were previous efforts successful? Why or why not?)

- *Do I know who else is working on it or has worked on it, or would be interested in working on it?*

Then suggest that the girls come up with a list of questions about their issue. This list will guide their research.

Time Crunch and the Power of Multitasking

Gently remind the girls of their time-crunch factor. For those with a tight time crunch, talk about the power of multitasking. The girls' book separates out Advocacy Steps 1 to 4—finding a cause you believe in, zooming in on one angle and one best solution to advocate for, forming alliances with partners who can assist with your advocacy efforts, and identifying the VIPs to whom you will present your pitch. For Ambassadors who have plenty of time, step-by-step is the best way to go. But those working in a team may prefer to multitask. They might think of their research as one big scavenger hunt that covers all four steps at once. They can even create a mini-chart, like the one below, to record their progress.

ISSUE	SOLUTIONS	PARTNERS	VIPS

Starting the Research

If you're in a location with access to research resources (such as a school or library), invite the girls to use the remainder of the meeting to start researching their issue. Make yourself available to guide their efforts, and encourage them to continue their research outside of the meeting. They'll want to be ready for the next session, which begins with an evaluation of their research. Emphasize that the type of research they're doing now is just one slice of a full research pie; solid advocacy research goes beyond what can be found on the Internet or in books—it means getting out in the community to talk to those involved with or affected by the issue.

If your meeting place doesn't have computers, the Internet, and phones, ask the girls to formulate an alternate research strategy. Get a brainstorm going to plan a road map for research that uses available resources and time outside of Ambassador meetings. Perhaps start with a group discussion about their research needs. Consider going to a library as a group, so the girls can team up on tasks and you can guide them to break down what needs to be done.

RESEARCH TIPS

Guide the girls to where and how they can find information—but not what information (that's for the girls to determine). Encourage them to talk about where they can get their information, who can help them, when they can do their research, and whether they will do it as a team or on their own.

This is where the government pages of your phone book will prove handy. Explain that it provides a "Cliffs Notes" of community contacts in the "government listings" (usually a blue or white section), which may prove to be a valuable resource.

For example, if a girl wants to advocate for a playground to be built on an empty neighborhood lot, direct her to the phone numbers for the Parks Department or City Hall, which she can call to gather information specific to her issue.

RESEARCH: IT'S A GIRL'S CHOICE

As the girls delve into their issues, they can pick one of the five research approaches detailed in "Step 2: Tune In" on pages 48–50 of their books. Each approach reflects a separate learning style. Based on what you have observed or know about the girls in your group, make recommendations as needed.

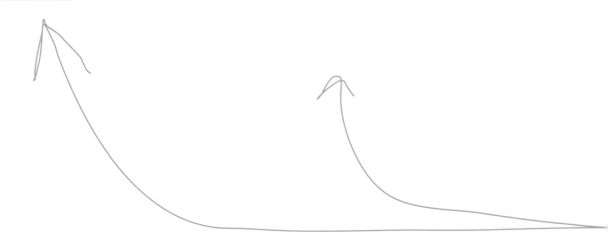

Take an Assessment Break

Once girls feel that they have accomplished a significant amount of research, ask them to turn to "Assessing Your Research" on page 52 of their book—questions meant to assist them in refining their issue and their solution.

Looking Ahead to Session 4

Suggest that one girl remind the group a few days ahead of the next session, via phone or e-mail, to bring in all their research notes and ideas. The girls will spend part of the meeting exchanging feedback as they consider potential advocacy partners. If the girls are multitasking, they may already be speeding ahead with identifying partners and even VIPs.

Discover Your Inner Child

Research can get heavy, so lighten the mood with the "Discover Your Inner Child" Take 5 activity on page 55 of the girls' book. Perhaps even share your own favorite inner-child activity! Of course, if you're meeting at a library, this Take 5 might be hard to do. So perhaps give the girls a few tips and let them create their own Take 5 break, based on your location.

Closing Ceremony (optional)

If the girls planned a closing ceremony or would like to create an impromptu one, now's the time.

Interesting

A is for acknowledge—that you've got an important job to do, and with this guide you'll do it well.

"To me, success means effectiveness in the world, that I am able to carry my ideas and values into the world—that I am able to change it in positive ways."

—Maxine Hong Kingston

SAMPLE SESSION 4
Building a Network of Partners

AT A GLANCE

Goal: Girls understand the importance of partners and have a plan to build their network.

(Experiences and discussions from Steps 3 and 4 of the girls' book)

- Opening Ceremony (optional)
- Marshmallow Madness (optional)
- Evaluating the Research
- Brainstorming Solutions
- Talking Points (or Scripting the Message)
- Who's on Their Lists?

- Take 5: Six Degrees of Separation/Team Builder: Building a Network
- Looking Ahead to Next Steps and Session 5
- Closing Ceremony (optional)

MATERIALS

- 1 bag of marshmallows (for optional Marshmallow Madness activity)

- Chart paper
- Markers

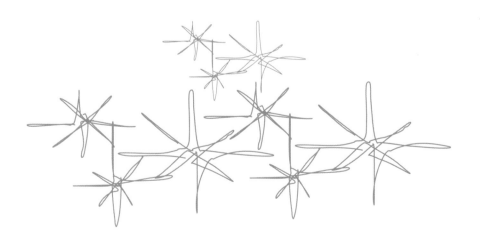

Opening Ceremony (optional)

Ask the girls if they want to do an opening ceremony of their choosing.

Evaluating the Research

Now's the time for the Ambassadors to share the research they've accomplished and to check in with one another on whether they've successfully zeroed in on one aspect of an issue and have proposed workable solutions that partners and VIPs will find enticing. To get the girls started, create a chart on newsprint with the following questions:

- Which research option did you choose?

- What was the most interesting thing you discovered?

- Did the research raise new questions? Do any questions remain unanswered?

- Did the research change your ideas about the issue? If so, how?

- Did the research spark ideas for solutions to the problem? If so, what?

- Have you focused in on one solution that you will now advocate for?

Girls working independently can take a few minutes to answer the questions. Those working as a group can answer them together (they can choose one girl to report on all of them or they can divide up the questions). If girls have additional questions or unanswered questions, ask them how they'll find the answers. Do they need any assistance?

Brainstorming Solutions

Now ask the girls to focus on the possible solutions to their issue. Do they have viable ones in mind? Do they need to brainstorm further? As the girls go over possible solutions, it's important that they keep these questions in mind:

- Is this solution a step toward a lasting impact? Will it contribute to movement toward long-lasting change? (Keep in mind the Butterfly Effect. What distant and long-term change can possibly result from the girls' small wing-fluttering?)

- Do the VIPs they eventually hope to pitch to have the influence to make this solution happen? (If so, zeroing in on VIPs can happen right now.)

If the girls have decided to work on one issue as a group, use chart or butcher paper for this brainstorm:

- Write the girls' chosen issue in the middle of the paper, and invite them to work as a group to write solutions (based on their research) that could create lasting change all around it.

If the girls are working independently on separate issues, do the same brainstorm activity using smaller sheets of paper or index cards:

- Ask that they write a phrase describing their issue in the middle of the paper and then tape it to the wall (spread out, so the girls can view it and comment easily).

- Invite the girls to do a "gallery walk" during which they write suggested solutions for issues on each paper. After all have circulated through the "gallery," ask the girls to take their paper down from the wall and review what others have written.

Lead a reflection discussion in which the girls review each solution and consider questions such as:

- Who will it help? How many people could I help?

- Will this idea make the biggest difference?

- Is this solution sustainable?

- Is this the most possible/practical idea?

- Will this idea involve the fewest decision-makers?

- How much time do I have? What is possible within this time frame?

- Will this require resources we don't have?

Based on their answers to each question, ask the girls to narrow their solutions to one best choice (or brainstorm new ones).

TIME WITH A PR PRO

This session offers a great opportunity to invite a local PR expert to be a guest speaker. She can share top "talking points" tips, assist the girls in writing their own talking points, give suggestions on networking, and offer her own career perspectives on persuasive speaking and writing.

PARTNERS AND VIPS

With the issue, research, and solutions fresh in the girls' minds, transition them into thinking about possible partners and even VIPs. Assure them that it's OK if they don't yet know who might be potential partners in their "Advocacy Network." Encourage them to think of people they may want to invite. Again, if the girls have chosen to multitask, they may already have a selection of partners.

PARTNERS are people who share an interest in addressing the chosen issue. They can assist in preparing the pitch and identifying and gaining access to VIPs. They may even carry forward efforts when the Ambassadors end their journey.

VIPS (Very Influential People) are those who can actually do something about the chosen issue. They are the movers and shakers who put things in motion toward the proposed solution. The Ambassadors and their partners will make the pitch to the VIPs.

Talking Points (or Scripting the Message)

The following "Talking Points" exercise will get the girls focused on their advocacy issue so they can communicate it in a brief and compelling way as they reach out to potential partners.

- Ask the group: *Have you ever heard the term "talking points"?*

- Depending on their response, you might share a brief definition: *"Talking points" are what people in the media, politics, and business call a short list of key points and summaries that convey a speaker's "agenda"—what she wants to get across to her audience. PR professionals, for example, might prepare talking points for clients to keep their presentations focused and forceful.*

- Then say to the girls something like: *It's helpful to think of talking points as an introduction, overview, and guide for how you will talk with potential partners as you reach out to create your network. You may also end up making use of your talking points later, when you write your pitch, which you and your partners will deliver to your VIPs.*

Ask the girls to divide into small teams based on the group's size. Provide each group with a large piece of paper and markers. Assign each group one category of questions to answer—What, Who, or How (if the girls are working independently, they can answer all the questions on their own):

- WHAT: What is the issue? What will I tell others about it? What is being done or has been done before? What solution(s) am I proposing (in other words, what am I advocating for)?

- WHO: Who will benefit from this effort? Who else is working on or has worked on this issue? Who are the decision-makers for this issue? Who has the influence to make the needed change happen? Who needs to know about my desire for change?

- HOW: How will I create change? How will I communicate my efforts to others? How will I encourage others to join in my efforts? How can I make my case?

Ask the teams (or individual girls) to reflect on the research they've done and answer the questions in their category. Emphasize that doing so will prepare them to answer any questions that may arise as they reach out to potential partners and, later, when they make their pitch to VIPs. The goal is to be as knowledgeable and focused about their advocacy efforts as possible.

As the girls write their answers, you can circulate and offer assistance as needed. When they're done, ask them to review their answers and then synthesize the information into three talking points that they might use with a potential partner.

- The points should take no more than 30 seconds to say (about 100-150 words total).

- If the girls are working in teams, ask for girl volunteers to chart their talking points. As they craft their points, maintain an active role in the conversation. Serve as a gentle "reality check" to ensure that their choices make sense.

- If the girls are working independently, after 5-10 minutes ask them to exchange their talking points with another girl and give each other feedback.

- Then ask the girls to refine their points as needed. Once their talking points are polished, they can use them to reach out to potential partners.

CONNECTING THE DOTS

This next activity covers the "Who's on Your List" and "Connect the Dots" sections on pages 60–61 in the girls' book. Invite the girls to use sheets of newsprint taped together (or rolls of butcher paper) so they can connect the dots to discover (or confirm, if they've already been networking) the best potential partners to approach for their advocacy effort.

Who's on Their Lists?

Ask the girls to go back to the "Community Connections" and "Building a List of Allies" pages in their books (pages 38 and 51). They'll see that they already have a full list of potential partners. And their family, friends, classmates, co-workers, teachers, coaches, and religious leaders may have connections to others who, in turn, are connected to still more others who might partner with them in advocating for their cause.

Say something like:

- *Now as a group, let's connect the dots of all our connections. Put a P by the names of potential partners and a V by potential VIPs. Once you gather with your partners, you'll assess possible VIPs more thoroughly, but this will get you started.*

- *Think of people you know of through friends, family, clubs, school, or organizations who have skills or experience that may be helpful for addressing the issue (such as a friend of the family who is a statistician, the journalism teacher at your school, or the worker at City Hall who knows your aunt).*

- *Remember your Girl Scout alumni network from page 35 and all of the people you have met in your research.*

IDENTIFYING PARTNERS

Ask the group to review the chart and answer the following questions:

• Who can best help spread the word about my/our issue?

• Who knows the most people in areas or positions related to my/our issue?

• Who shares my/our passion or interest in the issue?

• Who has a skill or talent that can best support my/our efforts?

IDENTIFYING VIPS

Ask the girls to identify at least two VIPs. Remember: VIPs are people who can take some action to move the proposed solution forward. If the Ambassadors are working as a group, suggest that they discuss the VIP candidates and come to a consensus.

Take 5: Six Degrees of Separation

For some fun, and silliness, try the "Six Degrees of Separation" game on page 64 of the girls' book. Or try the following more active version that lets girls easily see how connected their world is:

Team Builder: Building a Network

• Everyone stands in a circle.

• The first girl holds a ball of yarn and names someone she knows (who is not in the room), and anyone in the circle who also knows this individual raises her hand.

• The girl then holds onto the end of the yarn and tosses the ball to any of the girls who have raised their hands.

• The second girl names another contact, while holding onto part of the yarn, and tosses the ball to anyone who raises her hand.

• Continue until every girl in the room is linked to the web of yarn. Feel free to keep going to create a very dense, complex network.

Looking Ahead to Next Steps and Session 5

The girls now need to contact potential partners. Then they'll zero in on some solid VIPs—ones who can truly move their cause forward. As mentioned earlier, even though the girls' book separates the partner and VIP steps, this is a good opportunity for multitasking. If the girls are teaming up, this is the time to divvy up the list of potential partners so each girl can assist with making contacts.

- Talk about any planning they need to do, such as setting up a networking meeting of the partners to enlist their assistance as the advocacy effort moves forward. Talking with partners can also take place online or by phone.

- Identifying VIPs—a key role for partners. Their connections and the girls' add up to a whole lot of potential. The Ambassadors may not be able to reach all potential VIPs, but the point is to identify at least one or two to pitch to. Encourage the girls to review the list of possible VIPs on page 68 of their books.

- Time with partners might also include discussing the issue and refining the solution, as needed, and planning the pitch that will be presented to the VIPs.

Closing Ceremony (optional)

Save time for a closing ceremony, if the girls planned one. If not, consider adding reflection time for the girls to talk about where they are and how they are feeling about their advocacy efforts so far.

> ## BUILD EXTRA TIME
>
> If possible, you may want to add some time between now and the next session so that the girls have a chance to meet fully with their partners (or this could happen during an additional session), and perhaps hold a special launch meeting with them. Or ask the girls to chart out how they will identify partners between sessions. Either way, make sure the girls are comfortable with the next steps they need to accomplish.

PLANNING THE PITCH MEETING

In scheduling a pitch meeting with the VIPs, proper advance notice is key. Support the girls' needs as they decide on a meeting location, date, time, and purpose. They may need your assistance to secure a location or to identify a regularly scheduled meeting to attend, or to deal with basic logistics, such as transportation to the meeting place. Follow up as needed after the girls receive confirmation that their VIP meeting is a go. Plans may need to be adjusted based on the VIPs' responses and/or availability.

SAMPLE SESSION 5
Reporting Back on Partners and Possible VIPs, and Planning the Perfect Pitch

AT A GLANCE

Goal: Girls are ready and confident to present their pitch to VIPs.

(Experiences and discussions from Steps 4 and 5 in the girls' book)

- Opening Ceremony (optional)
- VIPs and Power
- Joys and Jitters of Public Speaking
- Perfect Pitch

- Perfecting the Real Pitch
- Looking Ahead to Session 6
- Ceremony of Hopes
  (and Closing Ceremony)

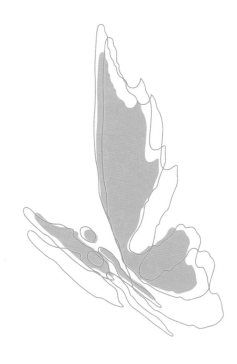

Opening Ceremony (optional)

Offer the girls time to perform any opening ceremony they had planned, or an impromptu one of their choice.

VIPs and Power

By now, having met and networked with their partners, the girls will have also zeroed in on their VIPs—especially if they followed the multitasking route suggested in Session 3. Perhaps they've even filled in the "My VIPs" section of Advocacy Central. Ask the girls to share their VIP lists to get feedback from the group. Ask: *How could their identified VIPs act on the issue?* If the girls are working in several groups, this is a good way to pool what they've learned from their meetings with partners.

Then transition the group to a discussion about the power and influence of VIPs. Ask for their thoughts about the kinds of people who have power on their issue. Possible answers include: teachers, parents, employers, heads of companies, city officials, and members of boards of directors.

Talk with the girls about how some VIPs, such as members of a board of directors, have a great deal of power over their organizations. They set policy and determine the group's mission and direction. They often also have the power to hire and fire.

Ask the girls to think about the various kinds of power individuals and organizations have, such as:

- **Positional power** (rank or title)

- **The power of knowledge**

- **The power of experience** (time devoted to a cause or profession)

- **Expertise** (skill and talent honed over time)

- **Star power** (using one's popularity/celebrity status to create media attention for a cause)

Ask:

- *What kind of power do your VIPs have in relation to your cause?*

- *If you have multiple VIPs, do they represent various kinds of power?*

- *Is there a certain kind of power you are missing in your VIP list? Is it important for your cause?*

Then transition the girls to a discussion of their own power. Ask:

- *What kind of power do you have?*

- *When have you felt powerful? Powerless?*

- *Can you give examples of using power for good? For bad?*

- *Is power a positive word?*

Joys and Jitters of Public Speaking

Now's a good time for a quick discussion of the Ambassadors' experiences with public speaking. Ask them to think about when they've been a speaker— and a listener.

Ask questions like:

- *What good (powerful!) experiences have you had as a speaker? Which were not so good?*

- *What types of speakers do you prefer to listen to?*

- *What lessons have you learned from your time as a speaker or a listener?*

Your own perspective on public speaking might be interesting for the girls to hear. After all, every time you meet with the Ambassadors, you are acting as a public speaker. What might you share with the group about your own public-speaking experience?

Perfect Pitch

Step 5 (page 72) of the girls' book offers detailed activities to help prepare the "perfect pitch" to deliver to their VIPs. Follow up on these by emphasizing two main points about planning a perfect pitch:

- Although the girls may be eager to "pack it all in" and give their audience as much of their research as possible, too much information, and too much talking—even if passionate and well-intended—will most likely result in an ineffective pitch. So encourage them to be brief and concise.

- Even the best and pithiest pitch needs to be aimed at the right VIPs. Addressing VIPs who can't act on the proposed solution or move it forward won't get the desired result.

Ask the girls to try one or both of the following activities (Pitch It and More Pitching Practice) as a chance to practice selling others on an idea in a fresh and quick way. These activities underscore how a successful pitch takes research, hard facts, support, and knowledge of the audience.

THE PITCH is a short and motivating presentation that is tightly focused on one aspect of the issue and a proposed solution that the identified VIPs have the power to put into motion.

Pitch It

Have the girls pretend they want to make a pitch to the school principal for fresh-fruit shakes (or another item of their choice) to be offered in the school cafeteria. What will their strategy be? Ask them to offer up their initial thoughts. Responses might include:

• Ask her when she's in a good mood.

• Get a petition signed.

• Refer to data on the healthful benefits of fresh-fruit shakes.

• Bring data comparing the cost of fresh-fruit shakes to other items being sold.

Then offer the girls this Checklist to a Great Pitch:

Prepare Your Pitch Early. Don't wait until the last minute.

Support Your Case with examples, benefits, facts, statistics, expert opinions, and anecdotes.

Make Your Presentation Pop

• Hook your audience right away: Tell a joke (if you're good with humor), bring a prop, be lively, tell a story.

• Keep your pitch clear and simple, building your case as you go.

• Know your audience: Be sure to say what's in it for them.

Practice in front of a mirror or friends to make sure you know your stuff and can deliver your pitch well.

Impress with Speech and Style

• Wear clothing appropriate for your audience.

• Act relaxed and confident (even if you're not) and make eye contact.

Ask the girls to take 10 minutes and create a "perfect pitch" to sell their fruit- shake idea (or another concern—even their advocacy issue, if they like, although that may require more time to prepare) with either:

• A one-minute verbal presentation (given individually or in pairs or trios), or

• A sketch of a mock print ad.

Then have the girls take turns making their pitch. The rest of the girls can play the part of the school principal (or whatever official body is being pitched to) and give a "yea" or "nay" vote (or something in between) and an explanation for it.

More Pitching Practice

Using the talking points the girls scripted in Session 4, this role-playing activity has one girl acting as a VIP (head of the local YMCA, city or town mayor, etc.) while another girl tries to enlist her support for her cause. Each girl should have a turn playing a VIP and then herself (representing her chosen advocacy issue). If possible, film or tape the girls so they can review their "performances." You can set up the activity so that girls:

- sit back-to-back and pretend to be on the phone

- sit face-to-face as though meeting in an office

- walk side-by-side as though meeting on the fly at an event

- stand next to each other as if on an elevator

Explain to the girls that an "elevator pitch" is one that can be delivered in the time span of an elevator ride. It has been said that major decisions made on the floor of the U.S. Senate and House of Representatives (and even in business) are often made "within the span of an elevator ride" as a staff aide whispers into the ear of an official headed down to the floor to cast a vote.

Perfecting the Real Pitch

Invite the girls to spend the next 30 minutes (or as much time as is available) refining their advocacy pitch. Encourage them to not only get their points down but to consider what questions might arise. What might their VIPs ask? Is there a particular avenue of questioning that's likely to come up?

Encourage the girls to work together as much as possible, even if they elected to advocate independently. For example, if a girl is creating a PowerPoint presentation or a speech, another girl can help edit it or provide overall feedback. So consider partnering them into teams for this.

If you are in a location that has computers, phones, and Internet access, the Ambassadors can "divide and conquer" right here and now. If those resources aren't accessible, provide guidance for doing as much as possible with pen and paper and for planning ahead for what the girls will do after the meeting. For example, if a girl plans to meet with an elected official, perhaps coach her as she generates a list of possible questions that may arise and role-play the meeting with her.

Wrap up the activity by suggesting that the girls create a to-do list of any final details they need to accomplish.

Looking Ahead to Session 6

Talk with the Ambassadors now about their ideas for "Closing the Loop" at your next gathering. Closing the Loop—Step 7 in the girls' book—is an opportunity for the Ambassadors to plan how they will keep their "butterfly effect" in motion even if they choose to end their advocacy efforts on their issue soon.

Discuss the possibility of inviting some or all of the partners to the "Closing the Loop" meeting (Sample Session 6). Partners could play an important role by offering perspectives on the pitch meeting and next steps. For Ambassadors who choose to end their advocacy work soon, partners might also agree to follow up on any next steps or unresolved conversations with VIPs.

Encourage the girls to think beyond the "big pitch meeting" by asking them to consider questions like:

- Which of our partners could continue the advocacy effort? What information could we give them? If not ourselves, who could we suggest the VIPs we are about to pitch to could call or follow up with to carry this issue forward?

- How could we connect some of our partners with each other?

- Do we know other Girl Scouts (even younger ones) who might be interested in some aspect of what we have begun? How could we get them involved?

- Do any (or all!) of us plan to stay involved as advocates on this issue beyond the time frame we had initially planned? If yes, what are the next steps for us?

- Who will we need to thank and share progress with after the pitch meeting? Can we start any plans for this now?

TIPS FOR CLOSING THE LOOP

The Ambassadors (and Girl Scouts as a whole!) will benefit by putting a little energy into "post-pitch" considerations. They would not want community members to feel that they started something and then left pieces of the effort dangling. So, before this journey winds up, you'll want to coach the girls to provide any basic follow-up they can to their VIPs, and to connect any work in progress to partners (people or organizations) who can take over possible follow-up actions that come out of the pitch meeting.

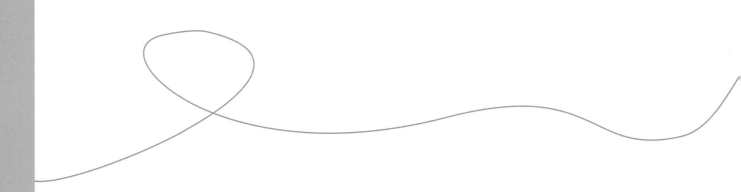

Ceremony of Hopes (and Closing Ceremony)

Even if the girls don't regularly have a closing ceremony, take some time to offer them a little confidence-builder in the form of a "hopes ceremony." After all, the girls are getting ready to go out and pitch their ideas to some powerful members of the community. Remind them how momentous this is. Ask them some questions, such as:

- *How do you feel about being assertive and speaking up for a cause you believe in?*

- *How does it feel to know you have been creative in finding a solution for a key issue in the community?*

Encourage the girls to discuss various scenarios of what might happen during the pitch meeting.

Then suggest that the girls perform a special closing ceremony today to commemorate how far they've come on this journey and what they've accomplished. They may want to add in some reflection time to talk about the skills they used or developed during the session.

MORE TIPS FOR CLOSING THE LOOP

If some of the Ambassadors have become invested in their issue and want to continue on as advocates for it, that's terrific. If you find that your own time is limited, talk with your Girl Scout council about other volunteers who might be able to step in. Perhaps you can even help recruit someone who started out as a partner! (Just be sure they officially register with and are accepted by the local Girl Scout council—for the safety of the girls.)

SAMPLE SESSION 6
Closing the Loop

AT A GLANCE

Goal: Girls identify the most important actions to keep a "ripple effect" in motion.

(Activities and discussions from Step 7 in the girls' book and planning for Step 8)

- Opening Ceremony (optional)
- Assessing the Pitch
- Capturing the Effort and Passing It On

- What Next?
- Planning a Closing Celebration

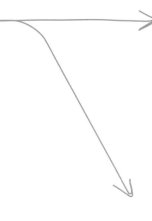

Opening Ceremony (optional)

Invite the Ambassadors to carry out any traditions they enjoy or have created to connect with each other and open the gathering.

Assessing the Pitch

Start the Ambassadors on a discussion about the level of success of their pitch meeting(s) with VIPs. If they have invited some of their partners to this gathering, this is a great time to also hear the partners' perspectives. If not, perhaps girls can share any partner feedback they received between the pitch meeting and this gathering.

Girls have some questions on page 91 of their book to guide them in thinking about their efforts to present their issue and solution to their VIPs. Here are some others to get the most out of the discussion:

- How effective was the pitch?

- What points seemed to go over well?

- What kinds of questions did the VIPs have?

- What aspects of the issue and solution did the VIPs seem most interested in?

- Did we choose the right VIPs for this pitch? Use the right information to present our case?

- What would have made the pitch meeting even better?

- If we had it all to do over again, what might we do differently?

- Do you believe your VIPs learned anything from your pitch about the issue or solution? Might they do anything (big or small) as a result of your efforts?

Capturing the Effort and Passing It On

Time and interest permitting, is there anything the girls want to create as an official "report" of their advocacy work? For example, the Ambassadors could:

• Write a letter to the editor of a local paper summarizing their efforts

• Get invited to a local radio or television station to discuss their efforts and progress

• Post a notice on a school or Girl Scout Web site or in a newsletter

• Create a photo essay or storyboard that describes the effort for display at a Girl Scout venue, school, library, or other community location

• Get together with other Ambassadors in their region to swap stories of advocating

The Ambassadors can use the research and ideas they gathered during all the steps of advocating and "boil it down." Capturing their effort could be as simple as creating their own short time line entry, following the examples in their book, or as elaborate as creating a short video describing the effort. Spending at least a little time summarizing how and why they chose their issue and solution, and their efforts to network with partners and "pitch" to VIPs, is a great way for the Ambassadors to reflect on what they have learned and to recognize the importance of their efforts as advocates—no matter how the VIPs responded. And, if the Ambassadors are in the mood to get a little artsy, this is a great time to create individual or team collages, songs, or poems that capture their efforts to raise their voices.

Passing Along Some Journey Knowledge

In addition to capturing their effort for themselves (and possibly a wider audience), the Ambassadors might enjoy "passing it on" to some younger girls. For example, they might want to share a few aspects of their advocacy experience, both the "work" of advocacy and their playful Take 5 breaks. Perhaps they could prepare a presentation on how to "break down" a project into its various steps and intersperse some "Marshmallow Madness" into it (see Session 4). This, of course, might call for adding on another session or organizing a "presentation day."

To get the Ambassadors thinking, start them off with this checklist, which they can elaborate on to fit their own presentation:

❏ **Identify an issue.**

❏ **Brainstorm solutions.**

❏ **Assess resources and find partners.**

❏ **Create a plan for change with your partners.**

❏ **Spread the word about your cause.**

❏ **Find those in positions of power to move your solution forward.**

❏ **Reflect on what you did and celebrate!**

What Next?

Remind the Ambassadors about the "Closing the Loop" conversation the team began at the end of Session 5. What loose ends can the team tie up before the journey ends? (Alternatively, if girls are continuing their efforts, here's where to start planning next steps.)

Invite the team to take some time to divvy up any actions they have decided upon to wrap up the advocacy effort and attempt to keep their "butterfly effect" growing. Will partners take on any follow-up suggested by VIPs? Who needs to know what? Do the girls need to send letters or make phone calls summarizing progress, key information, and next steps? Who is sending thank-you notes? Is the list complete? Now is the time to send out thanks!

Also, remind Ambassadors to update their lists of everyone they met along the way. This is a network they might want to tap for college and career information over the next several years! By saying thanks and tying up any loose ends, the Ambassadors will leave a positive and lasting impression.

Planning a Closing Celebration

Start a discussion (or invite the Ambassadors to start one!) on what kind of closing ceremony or celebration the Ambassadors would like. Perhaps they want one for just the team (for reflections and fun). Or do they envision a more formal gathering for partners and family members? Maybe they have time for a team retreat or party and a more formal event. Do they want to receive their awards at a ceremony? Do they want to incorporate a traditional flag ceremony? If they have decided to do a "Capturing the Effort" or "Pass It On" activity, do they see that as part of the closing?

If the Ambassadors have not yet had the chance to do so, a closing session could also be a practical gathering focused on exploring career choices related to advocacy. Ideas are offered on page 98 of the girls' book. Who might they like to invite to talk to them at this final gathering on the journey?

The closing session can be practical or celebratory—and formal or informal—or a mix just fit for this Ambassador team. And, if time is not a problem, schedule several gatherings and do it all!

Based on the team's ideas and resources, assist the Ambassadors to plan a ceremony or celebration that serves as a culmination to the journey (see "Sample Session 7").

"**I took the first step** and we are all marching on now to great achievements."

—Juliette Gordon Low

SAMPLE SESSION 7
Reflect, Reward, Celebrate

AT A GLANCE

Goal: Girls recognize their power to make a difference and inspire others.

(Activities and discussions from Step 8 of the girls' book)

- **Opening Ceremony**
- **Reflecting on the Journey**
- **Capturing the Effort and Passing It On**
- **Favorite Inspirations**
- **Award Ceremony**

This is the time for the Ambassadors to reflect on what they have learned and share their insights with family and partners. They may also want to receive their awards or share insights with younger girls at this time. What follows are simply ideas about what could be happening during the session.

congrats!

Opening Ceremony

Have the Ambassadors created a new tradition or loved an old one? Here's the chance to give it one last go—and even invite guests to experience it with them!

Reflecting on the Journey

By now the girls will have spent some time on the "Thinking Points" questions on pages 92–93 of their book. Ask them if they want to share their reflections with their guests or just with their group. Either way, they can go around and answer one question each—it's a good way to reflect on the entire journey and share their thoughts about it. You might add in some additional questions, such as:

- What was the best part of the journey? What was the hardest?

- If you were to continue working on the project, what would you do differently? (Would you change your proposed solution? Talk to more people?)

- What was the most surprising or interesting thing you learned?

- Did you develop or use a new skill or talent? If so, what was it?

- What action did you take that had the most impact or success? Why do you think it was so successful?

- What was the least successful action you took? Why do you think it didn't work?

- If you could redo one thing on this journey, what would it be and why?

- Describe the person you met on this journey who had the biggest impact on your advocacy efforts.

- Do you think you'll continue to be an advocate in your community and the world? Why or why not?

SHOW IT OFF!

The girls' reflections could happen on sheets of newsprint or posters, especially if they'd like to write down their thoughts rather than talk them out. Place a question on each sheet or poster board and give time for the girls to write their answers. Then give everyone time for a "gallery" review of what was "said."

Capturing the Effort and Passing It On

If the Ambassadors have created writing, videos, photojournals, or anything else that captures their journey as advocates, now is the time to show or unveil it! Or perhaps now is when they want to do some "pass it on" activities with younger Girl Scouts.

Favorite Inspirations

Perhaps the Ambassadors want to share favorite quotes or stories from women advocates across time and around the world—those they discovered in their books or on their own.

Award Ceremony

The girls can play up their award ceremony any way they like. Doing it up in a big way, with an extra session, is certainly a good idea—the Ambassadors have a lot to celebrate. Perhaps the girls want to present the Advocate Award to one another.

You might offer a few suggestions, such as:

* *After you present the award, say one "gift" you gave and got on the journey (for example, "I gave the gift of my passion and time, and got the gift of helping save the lives of animals").*

* *Then pass a candle around and offer a personal commitment to advocacy (for example, "I promise to always speak up for those who have been wronged").*

C is for...

Consider rounding out the session with a "**C** is for" ceremony, using the Girl Scout mission statement *(Girl Scouting builds girls of courage, confidence, and character, who make the world a better place)* and the lines on page 103 of the girls' book:

> C IS FOR COURAGE, CONFIDENCE, AND CHARACTER—AS IN THE GIRL SCOUT MISSION, AS IN *YOU*. AS AN AMBASSADOR AND ADVOCATE, YOU'VE GOT THOSE QUALITIES IN ABUNDANCE. SO C IS FOR CONGRATULATIONS! ENJOY A BIG ROUND OF APPLAUSE. MAYBE EVEN TAKE A BOW. THEN, GO FORTH! CHANGE THE WORLD A LITTLE MORE.

Or perhaps Ambassadors and their partners can come up with their own creative spin on the ABC's (or any other letter!) involved in being a Girl Scout Ambassador who advocates!

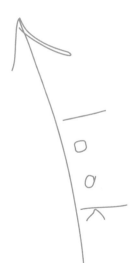

And Now, Take Time for Yourself!

Look back on the Discover, Connect, and Take Action reflection you did at the start of this journey (pages 30–31).

Were you successful in your efforts at guiding the girls to expand their networks?

_____

_____

_____

What about your own networks? Have they expanded?

_____

_____

_____

What did you learn along the way?

_____

_____

_____

_____

Think back to the first Take Action question: _Suppose this generation of young women were to put its advocacy skills to work in every aspect of their lives—how might the world be better?_

Has your answer changed at all?

_____

_____

_____

_____

 C is for *congratulations*— for a journey well traveled!